How many times have along than this"? Maybe you think your season has passed. Well, I have great news for you. Pastor Mia Wright has the refresher you need to ignite and inspire you to pursue your purpose right here in this book. Her poignant and practical insight has blessed millions on every continent of this world, and she has written this amazingly anointed book of rediscovery just for you.

Unthinkable is a powerful tool that will move you to action. Sometimes we need a push in the right direction to assure completion of the tasks at hand. You owe it to yourself to finish *Unthinkable* and then pass the knowledge on to others so they too can prosper in every way. Read this book and allow Pastor Mia to take you on this prolific journey toward what is actually thinkable.

—YOLANDA ADAMS
GOSPEL RECORDING ARTIST
HOST, *YOLANDA ADAMS MORNING SHOW*

Mia Wright challenges us to understand that although we may view ourselves as ordinary, God's view is quite different. She encourages us to do the unthinkable and walk outside the boundaries of ordinary and join hands with our Creator to do the extraordinary.

—JONI LAMB
HOST, *JONI TABLE TALK*
DAYSTAR TELEVISION NETWORK

It is *unthinkable* that Mia Wright wouldn't challenge you with this refreshing take on mastering the impossibilities in life, pushing the margins, and pressing beyond the norm. Mia is a woman who walks the talk and gives practical instruction based on experience as well as sound biblical principles. Get ready for a mind shift that is sure to change your life!

—MICHELLE McKINNEY HAMMOND
AUTHOR, *THE POWER OF BEING A WOMAN*

It is with great joy that I endorse this project by my dear friend and colleague Mia Wright. Since I met her (over ten years ago), I have known her to be a deep thinker, causing her to be cutting-edge in both her natural and spiritual leadership ability. It is no surprise that she would indulge readers in "the unthinkable." It is her mode of operation! However, what blesses me most is her willingness to share with all the spiritual revelation of why and how we should tap into areas of our minds, spirits, and souls to make the unimaginable possible! As we receive this incredible insight by faith, we begin to experience "more than we can ask or think" the Bible speaks of.

—DR. DEBRA B. MORTON
PASTOR, GREATER ST. STEPHENS FULL GOSPEL CHURCH
NEW ORLEANS, LOUISIANA

We are now living in a time when the atmosphere is filled with covert and overt messages that tell us what we cannot do. Limits are still being placed on us. Others are still trying to define us and thereby confine us. This book by Rev. Mia Knight Wright is a must-read for any woman who has lived by the boundaries others have established for her. It is fresh, relevant, insightful, and spiritually grounded.

As I delved into the content of this book, my spirit was lifted as I walked the journey with those who decided to not allow others to place limits on their lives. The book is unique not only because of the characters who were chosen, but also because the Reverend Wright lives by the title of her book. She has done and will continue to do the "unthinkable."

—Rev. Dr. Jessica Kendall Ingram
Episcopal Supervisor, First Episcopal District of the African Methodist Episcopal Church

Through explorations of the lives of biblical characters and challenging pearls of wisdom, Mia Wright has masterfully crafted an insightful, enlightening, and life-changing book that compels us to think large and unconventionally. Her personal and pragmatic reflections are rich in principles that inspire readers to know that the "unthinkable" is achievable when they move in faith. Read it and be blessed!

—Elaine McCollins Flake
Co-Pastor, Greater Allen A.M.E. Cathedral of New York

Mia Wright is a voice for all generations. In *Unthinkable* she makes us all think—and tap into the potential God has destined for us all. This is a must-read for you—and everyone you know!

—ReShonda Tate Billingsley
Author, *Let the Church Say Amen*, *Seeking Sarah*, and *A Blessing and a Curse*;
Publisher; motivational Speaker; Producer

UN
THINK
ABLE

UNTHINKABLE

MIA K. WRIGHT

CHARISMA
HOUSE

Most CHARISMA HOUSE BOOK GROUP products are
available at special quantity discounts for bulk purchase for
sales promotions, premiums, fund-raising, and educational
needs. For details, write Charisma House Book Group, 600
Rinehart Road, Lake Mary, Florida 32746, or telephone (407)
333-0600.

UNTHINKABLE by Mia K. Wright
Published by Charisma House
Charisma Media/Charisma House Book Group
600 Rinehart Road
Lake Mary, Florida 32746
www.charismahouse.com

Cover design by Lisa Rae McClure
Design director: Justin Evans

Visit the author's website at www.miawright.com.

Library of Congress Cataloging-in-Publication Data:
An application to register this book for cataloging has been submitted to the Library of Congress.
International Standard Book Number: 978-1-62999-502-1
E-book ISBN: 978-1-62999-503-8

18 19 20 21 22 — 987654321
Printed in the United States of America

Unthinkable is dedicated to all the women and men who thought their dreams were impossible yet saw them become reality, chief among them my mom, Barbara, and my husband, Remus.

CONTENTS

ACKNOWLEDGMENTS

I WANT TO EXPRESS my heartfelt thanks to a number of people who made this dream become a reality. Without your help I would not have been able to dedicate the time to complete this incredible work.

Thank you to my executive assistant, RoLonda Brown, who stepped up when I needed to step away from my day-to-day work.

Thank you, Kayla Adams, for being the timely vessel who reached out to me at the appointed time.

Thank you, Michelle Hargrove, for connecting Kayla and me.

Thank you, Valerie Lowe, for your listening ear, your input, and your words of wisdom.

Thank you, Kim Green, for inspiring me to share my story.

Thank you, Adrienne Gaines and the Charisma House team, for being a force for Christ and helping people live better lives.

And a special thank-you to my church family for giving me the space to write and understanding my absence, and to my Metamorphosis Alpha Team and board members for being so supportive of my endeavors. I love you all.

INTRODUCTION

un·think·able—(of a situation or
event) too unlikely or undesirable to
be considered a possibility.[1]

I HAVE EXPERIENCED SO many things in my life that I never would have thought possible or dared to dream. I was raised in a single-parent home on what some would consider the wrong side of town. Yet seemingly against all odds God blessed me to finish college with a degree in biology and chemistry, have a successful career in corporate and nonprofit sectors, marry a wonderful man, and raise children who make us both so proud. Today my husband and I lead a wonderful church, The Fountain of Praise in Houston, Texas, and I travel the world preaching and teaching God's Word.

At one time the life I now live would have been unimaginable to me. Unthinkable. Too unlikely for me to even desire. But God taught me that He is able to do "exceedingly abundantly above all that we ask or think, according to the power that works in us" (Eph. 3:20, NKJV). God did the unthinkable in my life when I decided not to settle for life as I had known it. I wanted more out of life than I had seen growing up, and as I placed my desire before God, He showed me how to break out of poverty and a self-limiting mind-set. He began to open my eyes to what He had in store for me, and His plans were beyond what I would have dreamed. I still cannot fathom all of what He wants for me, but I have learned to trust God with the things that seem impossible to me.

You see, when God began to show me His desires for my life, I began to study the godly examples of men and women in the Bible to discover my full potential in God. When I began to apply what I was learning, God began to do "exceedingly abundantly" above all that I could ask or think. And I was empowered to be my best!

As I studied these individuals, I noticed that they often did what others dared not do. They stepped out of their comfort zones and took bold steps of faith, at times defying convention and cultural norms, and their choices brought life-changing results. They did the unthinkable and experienced the impossible.

Many times we allow ourselves to live according to others' expectations of us. We let those around us or our circumstances define how far we can go or what we can accomplish. But it's time to rethink the boundaries you've set around your life. It's time to push the margins, press beyond the norm, and join hands with the One whose dreams for you are bigger than you think.

In this book I hope to inspire you to do just that. With help from the Holy Spirit, I have carefully selected ten biblical figures who broke from the norms of their day—most of them at great peril—to reach out to God in an unthinkable way. Some of their actions may seem small—taking a step, touching a garment, opening one's mouth to speak—but in each case God did something miraculous as a result.

Through these incredible stories of faith and action I want to challenge you to raise your level of expectation. My prayer is that this book will compel you to take a close look at your life and ask yourself some tough questions: Have I limited myself because someone said I couldn't do something? Am I holding back because someone said I shouldn't try something new? Have I talked myself out of going somewhere I have never been? If you are like me and most of the women I know, your answer to at least one of these questions is a resounding yes. But that can change.

You'll notice some patterns in the stories I'll share. First, you'll see that these individuals trusted God. This is because believing God is the bedrock of experiencing the life God desires for you. Only through Him are all things possible.

You'll also notice that each person featured in this book had a strong desire to get closer to God. These people weren't seeking personal aggrandizement, and neither should we. They allowed the Holy Spirit to guide their actions, not their own ambitions. Their focus was on seeking and pleasing God, not their community or the religious leaders of their day, and God rewarded them.

If you are tired of being restricted, this book is for you. If you have ever felt marginalized or been made to feel that your voice isn't powerful and important, don't put this book down. As you read *Unthinkable*, I want you to consider all the things you have desired to do but have been too afraid to try. Then ask the Holy Spirit to embolden you as He did the people in these pages.

Remember, these biblical figures are much like you and me. That's one of the reasons I chose them. They battled the same fears and hurts we face. But they faced them down, did things that were outrageous for their time, and experienced a supernatural result.

God wants to do in our lives what He did in theirs. He wants to heal our wounds, transform our marriages, save our children, bring us out of desperate circumstances, deliver us from bondage, and make us vessels of honor. Our God has no limits, and He wants you to let Him do the unthinkable in and through you!

I believe that embedded in the spirit and psyche of every individual is the desire to break out, to improve and be better. The problem is many of us don't know where we need to be or how to get there. This book will be your guide to move beyond where you've been.

Don't settle for the status quo. Don't think this is as good as your life will get. God wants you to reach your full potential in Him. He wants to do more in your life than you could ask or think. But in order to experience the change you seek, you may just have to do the unthinkable.

CHAPTER 1

UNTHINKABLE TRUST
MARY THE MOTHER OF JESUS

Mary responded, "I am the Lord's servant. May everything you have said about me come true."

—LUKE 1:38

⸻

S HE STOOD THERE alone, in awe, scared enough to run but unable to flee his presence. He had called himself a messenger from God and greeted her by saying, "Favored woman, God is with you." But it was all so confusing. "God is with me?" she asked herself. "What does that mean?"

She was still trying to comprehend the angel's words when he spoke again: "Don't be afraid, Mary…for you have found favor with God!" (Luke 1:30). Now she was both confused and disturbed. How did he know her name? Did he know her family too? Did he know she was engaged to Joseph? What could he possibly want?

As if he could hear the anxious thoughts racing through Mary's mind, the angel Gabriel began to explain the reason for his visit:

> You will conceive and give birth to a son, and you will name him Jesus. He will be very great and will be called the Son of the Most High. The Lord God will give him the throne of his ancestor David. And he will reign over Israel forever; his Kingdom will never end!
>
> —LUKE 1:31–33

She would have a son who would receive the throne of David and reign forever? It didn't make sense. "But how can this happen?" she asked. "I am a virgin" (v. 34).

The angel replied:

> The Holy Spirit will come upon you, and the power of the Most High will overshadow you. So the baby to be born will be holy, and he will be called the Son of God. What's more, your relative Elizabeth has become pregnant in her old age! People used to say she was barren, but she has conceived a son and is now in her sixth month. For the word of God will never fail.
>
> —LUKE 1:35–37

After that we hear no more objections from Mary. No more questions. She believed every word the angel spoke. Her greatest desire was to be part of God's divine plan, and she believed God was giving her that chance. So with a calm confidence she told the angel, "I am the

Lord's servant. May everything you have said about me come true" (Luke 1:38). I like the way her statement reads in the New King James Version: "Let it be to me according to your word."

It was unthinkable that Mary would respond with such trust. Nothing had changed in her situation. She was still a virgin. She was still unmarried. But instead of telling the angel all the reasons what he was saying was impossible, she chose to say yes to the unknown.

We have the benefit of knowing the end of the story. We know Mary gave birth to a son named Jesus, who willingly died on the cross to save us from sin. We know that Jesus's birth and death changed the course of history. But Mary had no way of knowing all that would happen. Nor was she fully aware of what would be required of her. She didn't know she would be ridiculed by her community or that she'd have to watch her son die a cruel, painful death.

But Mary didn't say yes because she had everything figured out. She didn't conduct a risk assessment and determine that the odds were best if she accepted Gabriel's words. I believe she said yes because of something the angel said: "For the word of God will never fail."

Trust is "assured reliance on the character, ability, strength, or truth of someone or something."[1] Mary may not have known how the Holy Spirit would overshadow her or how she would give birth to the Son of God. She may not have known how her cousin became pregnant after being barren for so many years. But I believe she knew the word of God could be trusted, and that was all she needed to know. With that knowledge, she was able to declare, "Let it be to me according to your word."

There was a time in my life when I felt uncertain about the future. During that season God spoke to me clearly about what He wanted me to do, but what He said seemed impossible. Interestingly I did not doubt for a minute whether God was speaking to me; I struggled with His message. I felt like Mary, wondering "what manner of greeting this was" (Luke 1:29, NKJV). I had no idea *how* God was going to do what He had said. But when, like Mary, I chose to say, "Let it be to me according to your word," God opened doors for me that I never would have dreamed possible. Through Mary's example I believe God wants to show us how to embrace the unthinkable life of trust He is calling each of us to.

GOD KEEPS HIS PROMISES

When we think of people God has called into His service, most of them are adults, but not Mary. She was likely between the ages of twelve and fifteen years old when the angel Gabriel appeared to her. You may remember Gabriel from elsewhere in the Bible. He is the one in Daniel 10 who fought with the Prince of Persia for twenty-one days to deliver the answer to Daniel's prayer. And while Zechariah the priest was serving in the temple, Gabriel announced to him that his wife, Elizabeth, who was barren, would bear him a son. (See Luke 1:5–24.) Now the messenger angel was standing before Mary to speak to her on God's behalf.

It had been four hundred long years since God had spoken to His people, which is why it was so remarkable that He would speak to a lowly Jewish girl. Mary was of no reputation. She wasn't born into some wealthy, well-known family. She was engaged to Joseph, but she didn't have a large dowry to present to him. Yet God chose to break His silence by speaking with her. If what God has spoken to you seems impossible or if you wonder why He didn't choose someone else to do what you're feeling led to do—someone with more education, better contacts, or more experience—you're in good company. Mary may have felt that way too.

Before the angel appeared to Mary, the prophet Malachi was the last person to receive a word from the Lord, and it wasn't a happy, feel-good message. The prophet had been instructed to tell Israel about the judgment that was to befall the nation because the people broke their covenant with God and turned to idolatry. The entire Book of Malachi is an indictment of Israel's wicked ways. The people constantly disregarded the commandments and continued to stray. Their unrepentant sin is what brought on God's silence. The One who spoke the world into existence in the Book of Genesis and who spoke to Moses in a burning bush had nothing more to say to His chosen people.

No one likes to feel ignored, nor does anyone enjoy seeking a response from someone who refuses to speak. It makes you question the person's concern. I am sure there were many people in Israel who felt forsaken because of God's silence. But I imagine it must have broken God's heart to not communicate with the ones He loved so dearly. God takes no pleasure in not revealing His plans for our lives, because nothing pleases Him more than having fellowship with His children.

But sin creates distance between God and His people. Isaiah 59:1–2 says, "Listen! The LORD's arm is not too weak to save you, nor is his ear too deaf to hear you call. It's your sins that have cut you off from God. Because of your sins, he has turned away and will not listen anymore." The children of Israel had turned away from God to serve other gods. That may sound like a problem that existed only in antiquity, but we do the same thing anytime we worship the creation instead of the Creator (Rom. 1:20). Whether it's money, a spouse, our children, entertainment, or a career, if we idolize it, it's a god, and it will block our communication with our heavenly Father.

Fortunately when we repent, our fellowship with God is restored, which is what happened to disobedient Israel. You would think that after going centuries without hearing a word from heaven, the people would have forsaken their silent God, but the opposite happened. During the silence the people repented and turned back to the Lord. To rekindle their relationship with God, they revisited the words of the prophets and read the Torah. And as generations of idolaters died, new generations of God lovers began to emerge.

At the opening of the New Testament, God's people were anxiously awaiting the fulfillment of the Messianic prophecies. They had studied the Word and knew His arrival would signify a new kingdom, one where their oppressor, Rome, would bow down to the new King of the

Jews. Their understanding of why He would come was wrong, as they believed the Messiah would be a political leader. But they knew their Messiah would come.

Paul wrote in Galatians 4:4, "But when the right time came, God sent his Son, born of a woman, subject to the law." Gabriel's visit to Nazareth signified that the right time had come for the Messiah to be born. Because Mary had grown up among people who were expectantly awaiting the Messiah, she understood whom God was sending into the world. But even she didn't understand the kind of deliverance the Messiah would bring.

We know from the Book of Genesis that sin entered the world after Adam and Eve disobeyed God by eating the forbidden fruit. Their rebellion cost mankind the intimate fellowship they had enjoyed with our Creator and their peaceful life in paradise. But even as God pronounced His judgment on all the parties involved, He also articulated His plan to make everything right.

God told the serpent: "And I will put enmity (open hostility) between you and the woman, and between your seed (offspring) and her Seed; He shall [fatally] bruise your head, and you shall [only] bruise His heel" (Gen. 3:15, AMP). Here God was declaring that a redeemer would be born through the seed of the woman. And though Satan would try to destroy Him, he would only bruise His heel. But this Redeemer would fatally bruise Satan's head.[2]

Notice also that Genesis 3:15 says "her Seed." Most of the time, "seed" references a man's offspring, but not here. Why? Because this redeemer would be born of a virgin.[3] Later the prophet Isaiah confirmed this when he

7

declared, "The virgin shall conceive, and bear a son, and shall call his name Immanuel" (Isa. 7:14, MEV).

When God broke His silence, He did more than speak to a young Jewish girl. He sent the Living Word, Jesus, whose presence changed history. He kept the promise He had made centuries before and used Mary to change the story for all mankind. I've said it before, but it bears repeating: God always keeps His promises. We can take that truth to the bank. When He promises to never leave us or forsake us (Deut. 31:8) or to love us with an everlasting love (Jer. 31:3) or to fight for us (Exod. 14:14), we can count on Him to be faithful to His Word. God is not a man that He should lie nor the son of man that He should repent (Num. 29:13).

Knowing that God keeps His promises is the basis for the unthinkable life of trust God is calling all of us to. But the fact that we can lay claim to God's great and precious promises doesn't mean life will be easy. Being part of one of the most important moments in history didn't protect Mary from suffering. Mary trusted God to bring to pass what He promised her, but that didn't mean she wouldn't face problems along the way.

When the Promise Causes Problems

Soon after the angelic visitation Mary went to visit her cousin Elizabeth. Some speculate that this may have been her parents' attempt to get her away from their community to hide her pregnancy. We don't know for sure why Mary went to visit Elizabeth, but we know God used this visit to confirm what the angel had said.

A few days later Mary hurried to the hill country of Judea, to the town where Zechariah lived. She entered the house and greeted Elizabeth. At the sound of Mary's greeting, Elizabeth's child leaped within her, and Elizabeth was filled with the Holy Spirit.

—LUKE 1:39–41

The moment Mary walked into the room, the power of God flowed through her to others. Mary wasn't perfect, and she wasn't deity. She was a humble girl with a willing heart whom God chose to bring the Savior into the world. The Spirit came upon her so she could accomplish what was humanly impossible, and that is exactly how He does the impossible through you and me.

Back in Old Testament times the presence of God remained in the tabernacle. But after Jesus died, He sent the Holy Spirit "that he may abide with you forever" (John 14:16, NKJV). The moment we are born again, we are filled with the Spirit. We get a new nature, and the Holy Spirit empowers us to live the Christian life. He's our prayer partner (Rom. 8:26), our Comforter (John 14:18), and our Counselor (John 16:7). He convicts us of sin (John 16:8), guides us into all truth (John 16:13), and so much more! It is impossible to live the Christian life without the power and presence of the Holy Spirit.

We need the Holy Spirit because as we're moving toward the promise of God, we will very often find ourselves face-to-face with problems. Trials and hardships will come, and when they do, God doesn't want us to think something strange is happening to us or that we are out of His will. The same thing happened to Mary.

When Mary left Elizabeth's house three months later to return to Nazareth, she was confronted with the reality that she was pregnant and unmarried. By this time it may have been difficult for her to hide her growing belly. Then there was Joseph. The Bible doesn't say at what point Mary told him about her pregnancy. It says only that Joseph knew, and he pondered what to do.

Joseph was a righteous man and did not want to disgrace Mary publicly, but no one could argue that he was in a difficult position. It must have been a struggle to believe Mary's claims. Joseph planned to break off the engagement quietly, but God intervened and confirmed Mary's story to him in a dream.

> As he considered this, an angel of the Lord appeared to him in a dream. "Joseph, son of David," the angel said, "do not be afraid to take Mary as your wife. For the child within her was conceived by the Holy Spirit."
>
> —MATTHEW 1:20

When God desires a plan to succeed, He will align all the details. God needed Joseph to be part of the story, so He revealed the truth to him. And Joseph believed, just as Mary did.

Mary had heard from God. Now Joseph had too, but the gossipers were still going to talk. People were going to snicker and question Mary's integrity and Joseph's sanity. The young couple faced some very real social stigmas, but the problems didn't cause them to doubt the promise.

I know this isn't easy to do. I know it's hard to trust God's promises in the face of opposition. But I have learned that sometimes God uses these problems to reveal His power to us.

At a time when my ministry was beginning to flourish and my calendar was filling up with speaking engagements, I suddenly felt weaker than ever physically. I had no energy and could barely make it through the day. I was exasperated and exhausted. I thought everything should have been perfect because I was doing God's will, so I began to question why I was facing so much opposition. I wondered if I was doing something wrong. In that season I learned that, in fact, I was doing something right.

In time I was diagnosed with Graves' disease, an autoimmune disorder that makes the thyroid gland overactive. My physician said I would live with this condition the rest of my life. But I believed my body was under attack, that the enemy was trying to oppose God's plans for my life. Instead of trusting in the doctors, I trusted that God wanted good health for me. I prayed and read every scripture on healing. Then one day the doctor told me the disease was undetectable. There was no evidence of it—no more indication that my body was attacking itself.

Through this trial, or test, I had to decide whom I was going to have the most faith in—God or the doctors. I chose to ask God what He saw for my future and trust Him with it, and He did what neither I nor the doctors could have done—He removed the disease.

Now when I face a problem, I know God is able. I don't hope God is able—I *know* He is. Had I not walked through my own trial, I would not have the same confidence I have today. The Bible tells us, "Faithful is he that calleth you, who also will do it" (1 Thess. 5:24, KJV). Problems remind us that only God can accomplish what He called us to do. And if He does the work, He gets the glory, which is the way it should be. All glory belongs to Him (Isa. 42:8).

With God the Impossible Is Possible

I find it interesting that we learn the most about Mary's encounter with Gabriel in Luke's Gospel. Luke was a physician by trade, which is evident in the number of details he includes. As a physician, he would have known Mary's story was scientifically impossible to prove. Dr. Luke knew where babies come from; he would have known it was humanly impossible for a virgin to have a child.

But Luke also knew what I have found to be true time and again: God has no limits. There is nothing He can't do. It may seem impossible for man to be made from dust, but we know that when we die, our bodies return to dust. It seems impossible for the solar system to have been spoken into existence, but even scientists and non-creationists agree that a "big bang" occurred when the right elements and gases collided. "Bang" always seemed like a sound to me!

It seems impossible for the Earth's rotational axis to be tilted and for it to complete a circle every twenty-four hours, orbit a sun that is 92.9 million miles away, burn without burning up, and not drift into orbit on its own or collide with another planet.[4] With the power to create mankind and to breathe life into His creation, God is more than able to do the miraculous. And yes, a virgin giving birth may sound crazy, but God can overcome physical limitations.

I sometimes have to remind myself how powerful God really is. I have on occasion encountered situations in which I needed more physical strength than I had. I remember the day my granddaughter's foot was stuck in a wrought-iron portion of a marble table. The table had been positioned in the same location in my home for more than ten years because it was too heavy to move. But the day she cried out because her foot was stuck inside the ornament and wouldn't come out, I said, "Jesus, help!" I somehow managed to flip this incredibly heavy table to its side to free her foot. I look at that table and often wonder, "Where in the world did that strength come from?" I know it was God helping me in my time of distress and need. There are countless stories like mine, of people having heroic strength when in crisis. In each of these cases I give credit to the One who can overcome every limitation in our lives.

God created our bodies. He knows every cell, tissue, organ, and body system that exists. He is highly capable of making each of these conform to His Word. If He speaks something, it will become a reality! The immaculate conception of God's Son, Jesus, isn't too hard to embrace once your faith is in the right place. If you trust science more than God, you will struggle. But if you believe God is the author of science and that scholars are still understanding His marvelous works, you will be able to trust not only that God allowed a virgin to conceive but also that He can still do the impossible today in your life.

Let me give you another example. Beginning when my step-daughter was young, she desired to have a family. The desire was so strong, I believe God put it in her heart. Unfortunately she was told she would never have children of her own. At twenty years old, fibroid tumors crowded her uterus and made conception medically impossible. That's what the doctors said. But today she is the mother of beautiful twin daughters, born from the same womb that was labeled infertile. And that was without taking fertility drugs or completing treatment for fibroids. God gets all the glory.

She wanted to be a mother, and she trusted that it was God's will that she would be fruitful and multiply. Her medical condition said, "Impossible." But she believed God said, "Possible." Everyone else said, "Unthinkable." She trusted God, and He had the last word. He gave her the desires of her heart. All things are possible to those who believe.

Mary's challenges didn't end when Joseph accepted her pregnancy. The social network of that day must have been filled with gossip and questions. People talk. How could anyone explain this? Angels weren't visiting everyone in town. Would the people of Nazareth accept Mary and Joseph's word that the child she was carrying was miraculously conceived? Or would the townspeople be as eager to stone Mary as others were eager to stone years later when a woman was caught in adultery? (See John 8.)

Over time I have learned to value far more what God says about me than what people say about me. Some people will never be satisfied with what you tell them. They will think something is wrong when all is well. They will turn over the proverbial rock in the graveyard trying to find dirt on you. It's so sad, but there are some people who will only see the dark side of things, and no matter how much proof they have that things are the way God wants them to be in your life, they won't believe it.

If you notice, Mary didn't surround herself with naysaying, unbelieving people. She wasn't even around Joseph until God told him in a dream that Mary was telling the truth about her unborn baby. If we're not careful and prayerful, people will make us doubt God, and before we know it, we no longer believe the promises and prophecies spoken into our lives. I no longer invest my time and energy into convincing people of things. I just continue to exemplify the goodness of God and walk in the power of His Word. I allow my life to be a living witness.

Unthinkable Trust Brings Unthinkable Blessings

I want you to think about the things God has spoken to you. Perhaps as children we heard God speak things into our lives that seemed impossible, unthinkable, too much for one person to accomplish. But deep inside we wondered, "Can this really be?" Or in different seasons

of life maybe God opened our mind-set to new possibilities and we doubted those things could happen. So
often we align all our knowledge against what God has
said, and we think what we heard can't come to pass.
But what if? What if we were to actually believe the
things God speaks to us, no matter how unbelievable
they seem? What if we were to take the limits off God
and off ourselves?

> For he took notice of his lowly servant girl, and
> from now on all generations will call me blessed.
> —LUKE 1:48

More than two thousand years have passed since
Gabriel appeared to young Mary, and today one of the
most common names for women worldwide is Mary. Two
millennia later Mary is still highly regarded as a woman
of faith, and she is perhaps the best-known mother in
history. Just think about that for a moment. Most people's names are erased from history. Their stories do not
outlive them. But not Mary. She has remained at the
forefront of history because of her unthinkable trust
in God. Her name has been referenced throughout the
ages. Her willingness to believe the impossible is still
being spoken of, written about, and widely discussed.
She believed what was inconceivable, and God used her
to change history.

When Mary said yes, God used her to bring forth
the Son of God. She became a vessel for God to reveal
Himself in human form. I believe that when we say yes to
God as Mary did, He does the same with us—He reveals
Himself to the world through our lives. What can God

do through you? What incredible history will God make in your life? You'll never know if you don't say yes.

In 1999 God began giving me indicators that my life was about to change. I will share more about this transition in a later chapter, but in 2000 I left my wonderful corporate job. I began to immerse myself in prayer to understand the next step for my life and what God wanted me to do. I wanted desperately to please Him and to be in His will. When I audibly heard God say, "Preach my Word," I had absolutely no doubt that it was Him speaking to me. The idea of women preaching was no longer foreign to me. The problem was I didn't trust that God could or would use *me*!

Because I came from a traditional Baptist background, I needed a paradigm shift to fully embrace this charge on my life. I needed to trust God like never before. I continued to bathe my life in prayer and to study God's Word. In fact, God showed me through 2 Timothy 2:15 that if I studied to show myself approved by Him, I would not be ashamed as I divided God's Word rightly. But it was Mary's words that resonated in my spirit: "May everything you have said about me come true" (Luke 1:38). Even when I didn't know how God would make His word to me a reality, I chose to trust Him and step out to do what He wanted me to do. And He has taken that yes and done more in my life than I could have ever dreamed. I have been blessed to preach around the world and to minister to you through the pages of this book.

Can you imagine the generations that will call you "blessed" if you say yes to God? It's time to challenge the unthinkable in your life and ask God to help you believe.

I am reminded of the man who brought his epileptic son to Jesus, saying, "Have mercy on us and help us, if you can" (Mark 9:22). Jesus didn't miss the "if you can," and He responded by saying, "What do you mean, 'If I can'?...Anything is possible if a person believes" (Mark 9:23).

The father initially cried out, "I do believe." But just then the reality of his doubts hit him, and he said, "Lord...help my unbelief!" (Mark 9:24, NKJV). With those words this man prayed one of the most powerful prayers in Scripture.

The man originally came to Jesus because His disciples hadn't been able to heal his son. This father wanted to blame them for the fact that his son hadn't been changed, but Jesus redirected his focus. It wasn't the disciples who had the problem; he was the one who lacked faith that God could do the impossible. With his simple prayer the father was acknowledging his own weakness. He humbled himself and recognized his need for greater faith, and his son was healed.

Remember, even a little bit of faith can move mountains. When you find yourself at a place where your faith needs to be strengthened, ask God for His help. He will give it to you. If you surrender your will and choose to trust Him, God will do the unimaginable in your life.

DO THE UNTHINKABLE

Trust and Obey

Blessed is she who has believed that the Lord would fulfill his promises to her!

—LUKE 1:45, NIV

When Mary visited her cousin Elizabeth, the Bible says the child leaped in Elizabeth's womb, and she exclaimed to Mary, "Blessed are you among women, and blessed is the child you will bear!...Blessed is she who has believed that the Lord would fulfill his promises to her!" (Luke 1:42, 45, NIV).

When I began to trust God, I began to experience blessings I never expected to see. As much as I loved my life before vocational ministry, I have found that nothing is more fulfilling than walking in my divine purpose. My corporate job was my place of preparation; it wasn't my place of fulfillment. I was just passing through and learning along the way so that when I got where God wanted me, I would be ready.

The Scripture says Mary was blessed because she believed the Lord would fulfill His promises to her. Trusting God is rooted in your ability to believe Him. No matter how impossible a situation may seem, the Bible tells us that all things are possible to those who believe.

But we must remember that blessings follow obedience. In Deuteronomy 28:2 God told the people of Israel, "You will experience all these blessings *if you obey the Lord your God*" (emphasis added). If we are to be called "blessed among women," as Mary was, we must be faithful to not only trust God but also obey Him.

God doesn't just want us to believe His Word; He wants us to act on it. When we do, we will experience blessings beyond measure.

CHAPTER 2

AN UNTHINKABLE CONVERSATION
THE WOMAN AT THE WELL

The woman was surprised, for Jews refuse to have anything to do with Samaritans. She said to Jesus, "You are a Jew, and I am a Samaritan woman. Why are you asking me for a drink?" Jesus replied, "If you only knew the gift God has for you and who you are speaking to, you would ask me, and I would give you living water."

—JOHN 4:9–10

I T WAS THE middle of the day, late enough for the morning crowd to be gone but too early for the evening throng to appear. So when she arrived at the well, she was surprised to find that she wasn't alone. A man was there, someone she hadn't seen before, and He was watching her. It wasn't the first time a man had stared at her, but this man's gaze was intense. She avoided making eye contact with Him, but His eyes kept following her.

She tried to focus on her task: drop the bucket in the well and fill the jar. But just as her bucket hit the water, the man broke His silence.

"Please give me a drink."

"He's talking to *me*?" she thought. He was Jewish; she was Samaritan, and the two groups usually went out of their way to avoid each other. On top of that men weren't allowed to speak to women without their husbands present.[1] His request was such a surprise, she found herself doing the unthinkable: she replied.

"You are a Jew, and I am a Samaritan woman," she said. "Why are you asking me for a drink?" (John 4:9).

Jesus's response was both intriguing and perplexing. He told her God had a gift for her and that He could give her living water if she would just ask. But He had no rope or bucket with which to draw water, and they were already at one of the deepest wells around.

"Where would you get this living water?" she asked. "And besides, do you think you're greater than our ancestor Jacob, who gave us this well? How can you offer better water than he and his sons and his animals enjoyed?" (John 4:11–12).

Honest questions deserve honest answers. Jesus told her that everyone who drank water from her well would get thirsty again, but those who drank His living water would never thirst again. The idea was appealing. After hauling gallons and gallons of water for weeks, she welcomed any alternative.

She wanted what Jesus had to offer because it would make her life easier. She had no idea that Jesus didn't want to just make her life easier; He wanted to change it completely, which is why He was about to confront her with the truth.

When she asked how to get this living water, Jesus asked her to go get her husband. "'I don't have a husband,' the woman replied. Jesus said, 'You're right! You don't have a husband—for you have had five husbands, and you aren't even married to the man you're living with now. You certainly spoke the truth!'" (John 4:17–18).

The conversation had taken an uncomfortable turn. She knew she was living in sin; everyone in her village knew the kinds of choices she'd made. That's why she came to the well at a time when she could avoid the crowd. That's why she'd love to get the living water this man offered—so she could avoid coming to the well altogether.

She tried to change the subject, to talk about church and the feud between the Jewish people and the Samaritans—anything to get away from the spotlight this man was shining on her life. But that wasn't going to work this time.

> Jesus replied, "Believe me, dear woman...the time is coming—indeed it's here now—when true worshipers will worship the Father in spirit and in truth. The Father is looking for those who will worship him that way. For God is Spirit, so those who worship him must worship in spirit and in truth."
>
> —JOHN 4:21, 23–24

His words were affecting her. They were sinking in, going deeper than the well she was standing beside. And she wanted it to stop, so she tried to end their little chat. "I know the Messiah is coming—the one who is called Christ," she said. "When he comes, he will explain everything to us" (John 4:25).

But Jesus would have the last word: "*I* AM the Messiah!" He said (John 4:26, emphasis added).

Could it really be? Had she truly been talking with the Messiah? His disciples showed up just then, confirming in her mind what Jesus had spoken. And when the truth dawned on her, she couldn't move fast enough. "The woman left her water jar beside the well and ran back to the village, telling everyone, 'Come and see a man who told me everything I ever did! Could he possibly be the Messiah?'" (John 4:28–29).

People came streaming to see Him, and she just kept sharing her story. The Bible says, "Many Samaritans from the village believed in Jesus because the woman had said, 'He told me everything I ever did!' When they came out to see him, they begged him to stay in their village. So he stayed for two days, long enough for many more to hear his message and believe" (John 4:39–41).

It was a strange request for Jesus to say He "must needs" go through Samaria (John 4:4, KJV) when most Jewish people went out of their way to avoid it. But Jesus knew He needed to have an unthinkable conversation with a woman of questionable character so He could reveal some truths that would set her and those in her village free.

THE TRUTH CAN HURT

Jesus's talk with the woman at the well is the longest one-on-one conversation He had with anyone in Scripture, and it is important for several reasons. In the Gospel of John, Jesus revealed Himself through seven "I Am" statements, and this conversation marks the first time He proclaimed Himself to be the promised Messiah.

By declaring Himself to be the Messiah to a Samaritan woman who was ostracized by her community, Jesus was saying that salvation comes through Him and that it is available to all, even people who are despised. But He was also affirming the woman's value. An unmarried woman who was living openly with a man who was not her husband may not have been held in high esteem by her community, but she mattered to God. In fact, she mattered enough for Jesus to go out of His way to have a talk with her.

To appreciate the significance of Jesus's actions, we have to understand the tension between the Jewish people and the Samaritans. For hundreds of years the Jewish people looked down on the Samaritans, who they believed didn't know the right way to worship God.[2] The Samaritans were actually born through the inter-marriage of the Jewish people and the Assyrians after the Israelites were released from Babylonian captivity around 538 BC. As the group repopulated the land, they worshipped the God of Israel, but they created a Samaritan Torah, which claimed the temple should be located on Mount Gerizim instead of in Jerusalem.[3]

Both groups believed they were right about where God should be worshipped, and the division grew so hostile, they avoided interacting at all costs. Samaria was situated between Galilee to the north and Judea to the south. But instead of cutting through Samaria to get to their destination, the Jewish people would go around because, according to the Levitical Law, Samaritans were considered unclean. Jesus would have known the Law forbade Him from having dealings with an unclean person, especially an unclean woman who had made so many wrong choices in her life. But Jesus went anyway.

The woman at the well is like so many of us who have made choices that left us feeling unworthy of a relationship with the Lord. I don't know how long the Samaritan woman had been in a sinful state, but I imagine the villagers showed her little mercy. She'd had five husbands and was making no secret of living with a sixth man she hadn't even married. They probably called her every name in the book.

It's easy to believe the negative things people say about us, especially when those words have been spoken for a long time. When we hear something over and over, it becomes ingrained in our minds. I am always saddened when I hear about women who have been marginalized by rumors. These women usually have amazing potential, but they allow what someone has said to keep them from fulfilling their purpose in God. It takes intentional effort to counteract the effect of negative words that get rooted deep into our thoughts.

When Jesus encountered the Samaritan woman, He set out to change the way she saw herself. He began by having a public conversation with her, which validated her worth. But He knew her life could change only when she embraced the truth.

It was God's plan all along for this woman to become an evangelist and lead others to salvation, but first she had to get real. Her credibility had been compromised. No one would believe a known sinner unless the woman owned up to her sin.

Jesus decided to use water as a metaphor. After all, they were at a well. So Jesus asked her to give Him what *she* needed most: water. In the Bible, water often signifies God's Word and the Holy Spirit. Jesus knew that though the woman had come to the well in search of physical water, what she really thirsted for was spiritual.

When Jesus offered her the gift of living water, she focused on the physical—that He had no bucket or rope and that they were already at a very deep well. When we have physical needs, it can be easy to think they are the most important things in the world. That is what was happening with the woman at the well. She was focused on how Jesus would meet her physical needs, not realizing He was really there to meet her underlying need for salvation.

In our modern society water is generally available. We turn on the tap, and out comes clean water. Even if we are away from home, we can purchase bottled water to drink. It is easy to think, our Western mind-set being what it is, that water is accessible to everyone on the planet. However, in some places, particularly in developing countries, this isn't the case. In some parts of the world getting water is still a chore.

I experienced this in Tanzania. Young girls in the village I was visiting, some of them only eight or nine years old, told me it was their responsibility to get water from the well for their families. They walked nearly a mile up a steep incline carrying five-gallon buckets on their heads. When they arrived at the well, they pumped the water by hand, filled their buckets, and walked back home. Then they did it all again the next day.

The Samaritan woman likely went through a similar process to get the water she needed to live. So it probably sounded fantastic to hear she could have refreshing water without having to get it each day from a well. "Please, sir," the woman said, "give me this water! Then I'll never be thirsty again, and I won't have to come here to get water" (John 4:15). She would no longer have to work so hard to obtain water. She wouldn't have to go to the well alone in order to avoid the other women. It was a win-win situation. Still thinking about her physical needs, she was all in, but Jesus shifted the direction of the conversation.

"Go and get your husband," He said (John 4:16). With those few words, Jesus forced her to face the reality of whom she had become and the problems in her life. Would she own the truth about herself, or try to cover it up with a lie?

Trying to save face is tempting when you're ashamed of something you've done. But the truth is we cannot hide anything from an omnipotent, omnipresent, omniscient God. He knows everything about us, even the secret pain we never discuss. He desires inner truth from each one of us. He wants us to be honest with Him and ourselves so He can give us the answers we truly need. Chances are He will not heal the things we hide. Psalm 51:6 says, "Behold, You desire truth in the inward parts, and in the hidden part You will make me to know wisdom" (NKJV).

It was a courageous and powerful moment when this woman owned the truth. No matter how many lies had come from her lips in the past, the moment she chose to drop the facade and come clean, the unthinkable happened. The truth set her free. I know it's hard to hear, but we have to learn to be truthful because the more honest we are, the more liberated we become. I'm not asking you to do what I haven't had to do in my own life. When you tell yourself and God the truth, He will transform your life from the inside out. John 8:32 says, "And you will know the truth, and the truth will set you free."

"I don't have a husband," the woman replied. And Jesus affirmed her truth with more truth: "You're right! You don't have a husband—for you have had five husbands, and you aren't even married to the man you're living with now. You certainly spoke the truth!" (John 4:17–18). That must have been painful and embarrassing to hear. The truth sometimes hurts! But we must deal with our reality, even if it's hard.

After being honest with herself and with Jesus, the woman did exactly what many of us do: she deflected. She was good at avoidance. She drew water at odd hours to avoid other women. She married and remarried to avoid the sacrifices needed to make a relationship work. She opted not to marry the last man, thereby avoiding the marital commitment altogether. Not surprisingly then, rather than dealing seriously with her truth, she tried to change the conversation. She asked Jesus a question completely unrelated to what they were discussing. She asked about church!

> "Sir," the woman said, "you must be a prophet. So tell me, why is it that you Jews insist that Jerusalem is the only place of worship, while we Samaritans claim it is here at Mount Gerizim, where our ancestors worshiped?"
>
> —JOHN 4:19–20

I can't tell you how often I have witnessed to people about God's love for them, only to have them shift the conversation. They start talking about denominational differences, past injustices by clergy, or what people wear to church. "Hypocrites!" they say. Listening to someone avoid truth is frustrating for me as a Christian and as a soul winner. But more important, it can be a matter of life or eternal damnation for the person with whom I'm speaking. I understand what Jesus likely felt when He was speaking with the Samaritan woman. He wanted to talk about relationship, and she wanted to talk about religion. He wanted to tell her how much the Father loved her. She wanted to steer the conversation away from her sins because she thought surely God could not love or accept her as she was.

When she asked about the proper place to worship, returning to the division between Jews and Samaritans, Jesus responded by circling right back to the message of truth. The time had come to set this woman free. He wasn't concerned about Mount Gerizim; what was important to Jesus was this woman's soul. He wanted her to worship God in spirit and in truth.

THE TRUTH CAN LIBERATE

The truth, as painful as it may be, is what allows us to become free of the strongholds in our lives. A stronghold is a mind-set that controls our actions, keeping us from experiencing the life God wants for us. Only the truth of God's Word can destroy a stronghold because it's the only thing that can break through the lies we have come to believe.

In order to be saved, we must accept that our sinful actions are covered by the blood of Christ at Calvary. There is no use denying that we have sinned; God already knows that. But when we accept the gift of salvation that Jesus died to give us, we are acknowledging that while those things are part of our past, they no longer define us. We can let those past sins go and embrace a bright and better future. The Bible says, "Anyone who belongs to Christ has become a new person. The old life is gone; a new life has begun!" (2 Cor. 5:17).

Jesus helped the woman at the well understand what she really needed. She believed her physical needs were more significant than her spiritual needs, but Jesus dispelled that lie for her once and for all. She thought her intimate physical needs were greater than her need to follow God, but He dispelled that lie too. She thought she could live on natural water, but He gave her living water. She was living on lust, and He showed her real love. She hid the truth with lies, but He taught her that truth is the doorway to an authentic relationship with God and freedom in Christ.

Maybe you have been in search of something or someone to meet your deepest needs. And instead of turning to Christ, you continue to try to fill the void with more of the same. If you can relate to what I'm saying, then the message for the woman at the well is also a message for you. The real deal is found only in God. Every relationship, every desire, every need can be met through Him and in Him.

You may have been talked about much like the Samaritan woman was. The whispers and lies circulated by people who hated you only served as reminders of why God could not love you. But the good news is God *does* love you! Despite your bad decisions, terrible attitude, confusion, hurt, and pain, He still loves you with an unconditional love that can change your life. His truth is bound up in His love for you. It can transform your life if you accept it freely.

God's truth can help you reprioritize your agenda. The woman went to the well because she needed water. After encountering the Living Water, she left her water jar and ran into town to share with others the good news she had discovered.

When we face the truth about ourselves and allow that truth to set us free from past hurt and pain, we can restructure the priorities in our lives. What seemed important at one time may not actually be important at all after we are free! There is nothing more powerful than allowing God to take charge of your life and set in place the things that are of great importance to Him.

Maybe He wants you to be a missionary in your community and reach your neighbors for Christ. Or maybe He wants you to start a business or go back to college. God has plans for your life, and He is using the story of the woman and the well to get your attention so you'll move forward in the destiny He has for you.

THE TRUTH CAN RESTORE

I love the fact that the Samaritan woman's story did not end at the well. She had to share her experience with others—in fact, with everyone in her community. In effect, Christ made this "unworthy" woman the first evangelist to Samaria. He gave her a voice with which to share the gospel.

As women, we often share much of what's happening in our lives with close friends. I know I do. A woman's big "news" can be a new restaurant, new makeup, or even a new relationship. And we are usually expressive in what we say. We don't have to use a lot of words; we can express ourselves with a look or by using a particular tone of voice. For example, a woman can say one word such as "girl" or "hey" and mean a variety of things. Depending on how the word is said, it can reveal an innovation or express a broken heart; it can convey disappointment or excitement.

The woman at the well probably had told lots of stories about men, but there was a noticeable difference in the story she was telling this time. It was not about "a man" but about "the Man" who had been prophesied about for years. When this woman began to share what she had experienced, even the men of the town believed her. God gave her influence and expanded her witness when He restored her voice and her sense of value as a person.

Being silenced or marginalized because of who you are, what you are, or what you have done is a hard fact of life. Unfortunately people judge others by their actions, their reputations, and their history. The woman at the well was a sinner. We don't know what happened to her husbands, but she was living with a man who wasn't her spouse, which was forbidden by Mosaic Law. She was not only ceremonially unclean as a Samaritan but also morally unclean. Thank God for Jesus! He saw beyond all her faults and saw her needs.

Jesus transformed her life with a conversation, and she, in turn, talked about *Him*. She found her voice.

I remember when my son turned two years old and started putting together sentences to convey his thoughts. He had already been uttering words, but it seemed that we needed a baby translator to decipher what he was saying. One day the words started to sound clear, and with a bit of self-confidence he began talking like never before. I bought him a T-shirt that said "I just started talking and I can't shut up." As funny as the quote was, it was also very true. It expressed the sentiments of a toddler who had learned how to speak. His ability to express himself was a game changer. We no longer had to guess what he was saying. My toddler had tapped into the power of his voice. And since he started talking, he hasn't stopped.

Imagine how this woman felt when her voice was restored. Yes, she was new in Christ, but she was still telling people about Jesus. She was talking, and people were listening! She was no longer being marginalized or ignored. Her voice was being heard!

When she shared her story, people came out to hear Jesus. Her question, "Can this be the Messiah?," drew the crowds to Him. They were now listening to the woman they had marginalized. We know this because they told her, "Now we believe, not just because of what you told us, but because we have heard him ourselves. Now we know that he is indeed the Savior of the world" (John 4:42). Her changed life empowered her witness and her voice.

What are you called to share? What power does God want to release through your voice? If you believe the truth of God's Word, then live it. Speak it. Become an advocate for the truth, and let God use your life to change others.

Do the Unthinkable

Have a Talk With God

> My heart has heard you say, "Come and talk with me." And my heart responds, "Lord, I am coming."
> —Psalm 27:8

"You pray *every* day?" The surprise in her voice almost made me chuckle.

"Yes, I do," I said. "All throughout the day I'm praying in some form."

A lot of people complicate prayer, but there's nothing difficult about it. Prayer is simply a conversation with God, just like the woman at the well had. The only difference is that we don't see Him quite as easily as she did. She didn't have to wear special clothes or clasp her hands in order for Jesus to hear her. She needed only to open her mouth and talk to Him. That's what prayer is like for us.

When this young lady asked me if I got on my knees every time I prayed, I told her that I simply talk with God as I would talk with a friend, and when I come before Him, I feel His presence. Sometimes I go to Him with something on my mind and He gives me direction. Other times I just listen, and He encourages me.

God still longs to talk with us, just as Jesus talked with the woman at the well. He still wants to change us with His life-giving truth. We need only stop and respond to His invitation to commune with Him.

Have you talked with your heavenly Father today? If not, take a minute now to tell Him what's on your heart. He is listening.

CHAPTER 3

UNTHINKABLE COURAGE
THE DAUGHTERS OF ZELOPHEHAD

*The daughters of Zelophehad…came forward and stood
before Moses, Eleazar the priest, the leaders and the
whole assembly at the entrance to the tent of meeting.*

—Numbers 27:1–2, niv

T HE MINUTE THEY stepped forward, the sisters felt
the cold stares of the crowd.

The entire community was gathered at the entrance
to the tabernacle, with the leaders of the camp prepared
to conduct serious business—business that would affect
families for generations. Front and center were the representatives from the twelve tribes of Israel; Eleazar the
priest and the other chieftains; and, of course, Moses,

their leader. Then the sisters stepped forward, the only women to come before this group of men.

I can only imagine how intimidated they must have felt. Mahlah, Noah, Hoglah, Milcah, and Tirzah, the daughters of Zelophehad, were there uninvited. They knew what was proper; all the cultural dos and don'ts had been pounded into their heads. They knew this was not done—ever. But something inside wouldn't let them run away. The sisters weren't there to prove a point. They simply wanted to lay claim to what was rightfully theirs.

Their hearts may have been pounding, their knees shaking, and their voices trembling, but they courageously stated their case:

> "Our father died in the wilderness," they said. "He was not among Korah's followers, who rebelled against the LORD; he died because of his own sin. But he had no sons. Why should the name of our father disappear from his clan just because he had no sons? Give us property along with the rest of our relatives."
> —NUMBERS 27:3–4

Maybe the words didn't come out exactly as they practiced them, but these five women showed up where they weren't supposed to be and spoke up when they should have been silent. Instead of bowing to fear, they united as sisters to stake a claim to the promise of God. Maybe it was sheer desperation that caused them to show up, or maybe they wanted to set the record straight regarding their father's name. Whatever their reason, they took a bold step of faith in a time when women were not afforded the same rights as men. And because of their courage God was about to do something powerful.

> So Moses brought their case before the LORD and the LORD said to him, "What Zelophehad's daughters are saying is right. You must certainly give them property as an inheritance among their father's relatives and give their father's inheritance to them.
>
> "Say to the Israelites, 'If a man dies and leaves no son, give his inheritance to his daughter. If he has no daughter, give his inheritance to his brothers. If he has no brothers, give his inheritance to his father's brothers. If his father had no brothers, give his inheritance to the nearest relative in his clan, that he may possess it. This is to have the force of law for the Israelites, as the LORD commanded Moses.'"
>
> —NUMBERS 27:5–11, NIV

The audacity of these five women to step up and make a bold request changed their lives—and the lives of women in Israel for generations to come.

THE POWER OF SHOWING UP

Are you aware of the power of your presence? Before you were even formed in your mother's womb, God knew you and had a plan for your life. When He made you, He gave you all the gifts and talents you would need to fulfill His purpose for your life. You were born for this time for a particular reason. No matter who you are, no matter what your strengths and weaknesses are, you can transform the world around you—if you have the courage to show up!

So often we sense that God wants to do something new in or through us. We feel discontent, a discomfort with the status quo, but we talk ourselves out of doing something about it. We think of all the reasons we shouldn't go into uncharted territory—why we shouldn't lead the Bible study, why we shouldn't apply for the promotion, why we shouldn't go back to school, why we shouldn't address that problem in our communities. We fear rejection, failure, or ridicule, so we don't step into the unknown. Those fears are keeping doors shut in our lives. Rather than thinking ourselves out of "showing up," God wants us to be willing to go wherever He leads us, even if it's someplace we've never been or into an arena we think we're not qualified for.

Zelophehad's daughters had no examples to emulate. No other group of women had individually or collectively petitioned Moses, the priest, and the chieftains as they had planned to do, but that did not stop them. We now have their example to follow, but God doesn't want us running off into things He never called us to pursue. When we're thinking about "showing up" to, perhaps, start a new business or challenge a system or move into a new field, there are three things we must consider: our intention, our motive, and our direction. While your direction may be uncertain, your intention must be clear, and your motive, godly.

What do you hope to achieve? That is your intention. You should know what you intend to accomplish by showing up. Then, what is your motive? That is the why behind your intention. Why do you hope to accomplish this? The daughters of Zelophehad felt they deserved the inheritance that would have been given to their father. I always do a self-check on my motive, asking God if I'm doing something He wants for me. And then I wait for His answer.

Last, you must know your direction. How will you accomplish what you seek to do? What steps will you take? Most of the time you will not know all the steps, just the first one: the step of faith to "show up." For you, "showing up" may mean taking the GRE to prepare for graduate school. Or it may mean creating a business plan or applying for that promotion. The first step may seem small, but when God is leading, that first step will lead to another then another until you are exactly where God wants you to be.

It is impossible for us to fully know the depth of what God will do through us when we show up ready and willing to follow His lead. Even in a place that seems foreign, God can do the unthinkable. The daughters of Zelophehad lived exactly when they were supposed to live to accomplish what they were supposed to accomplish. They were part of a greater plan that manifested in its proper time, and the same is true for you and me.

Five Extraordinary Ordinary Women

In Genesis 12 God spoke to a man named Abram and told him to leave his family and go to a place God would show him. In time God changed Abram's name to Abraham and promised him that his descendants would become a great nation and inherit a particular land. God kept His promise, and hundreds of years later Abraham's descendants stood ready to take possession of the land God said He would give them.

Although no one had seized the promise, the land had been apportioned and the boundaries established. Moses would divide the land according to each tribe. Each tribe would divide its allotment of land to each clan. And the clans would divide it among the families, apportioning it to the fathers, who in time would pass the land on to their sons. There was no provision for land to pass to a man's daughters. A woman was expected to marry and then occupy the land her husband had been given. That's the way things were—until something unthinkable happened. "They" showed up.

Five fatherless, brotherless women stood at the entrance to the Tent of Meeting before Moses and the whole assembly and spoke up. One of the things I like about this account is that the Bible never indicates who spoke first, if they spoke together, or if there was one spokesperson for the entire group. It simply says, "They said."

The unity of this group makes a powerful statement. Being in one accord is a major accomplishment for any diverse group in any time period because there is power in agreement. Ecclesiastes 4 says, "Two are better than one, because they have a good reward for their labor....A threefold cord is not quickly broken" (vv. 9, 12, NKJV).

In unity these women did something remarkable in their day, but they weren't so different from you and me. When we take a close look into the meanings of their

Hebrew names, we gain insight into their character and discover that you don't have to be extraordinary to have unthinkable courage. Their names give us a peek into their lives and the obstacles they may have had to overcome to show up when it counted.

Mahlah

The first woman mentioned by name was Mahlah, which means "sickly," "faint," or "in pain."[1] Mahlah may have been similar to women you know who have had their share of physical illnesses, emotional pain, and mental stress and anxiety. She could have been dealing with psychosomatic illnesses, thinking she's sick and thus making herself sick. Or she could have been struggling with excruciating chronic pain. Either way, her name suggests she was weak and had some kind of health issue.

Although she was probably the eldest, she likely wasn't the strongest sister or the one everyone depended on—but she showed up. I can imagine that on the day they were to go to the Tent of Meeting, Mahlah chose to pull herself together and press through the pain to get dressed and stand before Israel's leaders. She had to let go of the mental and emotional anguish that had become a constant part of her life because the stakes were too high to let the pain stop her.

You may not be dealing with a physical illness, but you may have to press through difficult circumstances to "show up." When our problems are big, sometimes they're all we see. But there is more beyond that situation. There is a bigger picture God wants us to see. The promise God has for you—whether it's a material or spiritual blessing, or a new level of influence—may be waiting on the other side of that circumstance, so you can't let it stop you.

When your problems are big or your situation seems impossible, you have to get your eyes off the circumstance and onto God. Remind yourselves of the promises God has given us in His Word. Remind yourself of the things He has spoken to you in prayer or Bible study. If you fix your attention on things that will remind you that God is bigger than your situation and that He's able to do the impossible, you will begin to see beyond your own pain. That's what Mahlah did. She pushed through her problems and pain to show up and claim her inheritance. But she didn't show up alone.

Noah

Mahlah, the sickly one, stood with her sister Noah, whose name means "shaking" or "motion."[2] Noah may have been the sister who was always on the move. Maybe she was the one who was super busy, or perhaps she often wandered off alone. Whatever the case, I believe Noah's life was constantly in motion. We all know people like that, those who can't stay still for long. These are our multitasking, goal-busting, mission-minded sister-friends who always have two or three things going on at the same time. Noah was busy. Her mind was racing. She had things to do. And while she may have been quite accomplished, I believe some of this shaking and motion manifested negatively in her life.

Noah was born while the nation of Israel was wandering in the wilderness, and I believe her name may have characterized a life of instability. Imagine a table leg that is off balance and wobbles every time you lean on it or a washing machine that isn't level and rocks during every spin cycle. Maybe you have friends like this, or maybe this sounds like you. Noah's challenge was to focus on this one very important task and not worry about all the other things vying for her attention. She couldn't spend her time engaged in other activities when this situation needed her focus.

Research has shown that multitasking isn't good for our brains. According to Health.com, "It's not nearly as efficient as we like to believe, and can even be harmful to our health."[3] Yet we all do it. When I am honest with myself, I realize that if I had focused on one or two tasks, I would have experienced a better outcome. But all too often I opt for quantity over quality.

If you are like me and have been multitasking for decades, the good news is that new habits can be formed. The key is in learning to prioritize and setting healthy boundaries at work and at home. When I set priorities and create deadlines to accomplish what is most important, I seem to get more done in a timely and efficient manner.

Life may not have been in perfect balance for Noah, but she knew what to make a priority. She put her focus on the right thing at the right time. And when she needed to show steadiness and solidarity with her sisters, she showed up at the Tent of Meeting with the right disposition at the right time.

Hoglah

The third sister was Hoglah. There isn't much information regarding the significance of her name beyond its association with the partridge.[4] Aside from a reference in the well-known Christmas carol "The Twelve Days of Christmas," there's very little remarkable about a partridge. Unlike the peacock, with its colorful feathers, or the mocking bird, which can imitate the songs of other birds, the partridge is rather innocuous. Beyond a loose association with fertility, it is best known for the foolishness it exhibits in the wild.[5]

The partridge has been known to carelessly lay its eggs, often leaving them unattended. And it sometimes takes the eggs of other birds and tries to hatch them.[6] The prophet Jeremiah compared the unscrupulous actions of the degenerate to the partridge: "As a partridge that hatches eggs which it has not laid, so is he who makes a fortune, but unjustly; in the midst of his days it will forsake him, and in the end he will be a fool" (Jer. 17:11, NASB).

Because siblings are typically listed in Scripture according to their birth order, a light bulb went off in my mind when I realized Hoglah was likely the middle child. I began to wonder if her birth order may have played a role in her personality. Middle children often feel ignored. They don't believe they get the same attention as an older or younger sibling, and sometimes they feel they are in competition with their siblings—trying to keep up with the older one while trying to stay ahead of the younger. It's a conundrum that causes middle children to struggle in establishing their own identity.

As I considered what is known as the "middle child syndrome," suddenly it made sense why Hoglah's name is associated with a bird that seems insignificant and foolish. When people feel invisible, unloved, or unappreciated, they can become attention seeking. Seeking to gain love and appreciation, they can make foolish decisions and take careless actions. I wondered if maybe this type of foolish, competitive, or careless living characterized Hoglah's life. Maybe she had some deep-seated issues that made her do things to be noticed instead of exercising wisdom.

If you've ever met a person who had great intellect and little common sense, you may have met a Hoglah. When our actions are repeatedly unproductive or even harmful to others, it's time to consider what's motivating us. Living carelessly and not taking responsibility will have a detrimental effect because our actions always have consequences. God has a good plan for our lives, but we can sabotage those plans with foolish decisions.

A Hoglah's challenge is to seek love and approval from God and to let Him change the way she sees herself. New behavior patterns develop out of new thinking. Doing something different may feel awkward at first, but if you practice something consistently, it will become a way of life. When a Hoglah-type person recognizes her value in God, her actions will follow, and she will be able to pursue His best for her life instead of what gets people's attention.

When the time came for Hoglah to show up at the Tent of Meeting, she rose to the occasion. She didn't show up to show out, and she didn't distract from the sisters' mission. She put foolishness to the side to lay claim to what God wanted not just for her sisters but also for her.

And when she did, something interesting happened: the elders saw her—and they heard her request.

Milcah

Next there was Milcah. She likely stood out from among her sisters since her name means "queen."[7] Nearly every family has at least one child who is known for her style and her presence, the one who manages to always be the center of attention. She may have been the cheerleader, the homecoming queen, the fashionista, the social butterfly, or the high-maintenance sister who required far more attention and time than the others. But Milcah's name also means "counsel."[8] So in addition to being physically attractive, she also may have been a leader because people valued her advice and respected what she thought.

In my experience I have found that women who are leaned upon for advice, guidance, and leadership often have powerful public images, yet they face internal struggles that they rarely address. For a variety of reasons they do their best not to show weakness or vulnerability. They seek to be strong for everyone else, which eventually leaves them feeling drained. Behind the scenes they can begin to believe no one cares about what they go through, which can further prevent them from sharing their true feelings. I imagine that even in her time Milcah faced some of these struggles too.

Being "the strong one" often creates an unhealthy sense of responsibility, and it is only when the person breaks down physically or emotionally that she realizes she doesn't actually have superhuman strength. It is important that women who are carrying heavy responsibilities find ways to share the workload. Empowering others to take on some of the responsibility does not diminish your value in any way. In fact, it adds to your life. First, you are helping others learn by giving them the opportunity to exercise their gifts and talents. Second, you are freeing yourself up to take care of other important items. No matter how great you are at your work, you are going to get tired and worn down. Don't wait until your body rebels. Seek help! Pray and ask God to show you how you can lighten your load.

It is also imperative that women who carry a lot of responsibility find or create safe spaces to share their concerns. That can be with a counselor, a pastor, or even a confidante who is a good listener. Having someone trustworthy to confide in can help you think through some of your responsibilities and burdens.

Although Milcah may have been the most courageous and outspoken of the five, the Bible doesn't suggest that she overshadowed anyone that day at the Tent of Meeting. She knew their petition wasn't about one woman; their mission was to claim the inheritance they believed God desired to give all of them. So instead of showing up and taking over, Milcah lent her strength to her sisters.

Tirzah

The last of the five women was Tirzah, whose name means "favorable."[9] I see her as the likable one in the family, the sister whose presence drew others to her. She was the one everyone gravitated toward and with whom people could genuinely connect. Conversations with Tirzah were easy, as her welcoming personality was attractive and her calm demeanor refreshing. Very likely Tirzah, the baby of the family, was everyone's best friend. She was fun to be with and was probably always invited to events. Her name implies delight, which seems wonderful, but in reality, being liked by everyone has its challenges. It can lead to a people-pleasing disposition that can be noxious to an individual.

People pleasing can lead to life struggles that are seldom overcome without hurt and pain. People pleasers want to be true to themselves but all too often deny their own wants and needs to satisfy others' desires. They affirm the greatness in those around them, but they miss the greatness within. The pain of sacrificing themselves to please others is sometimes masked by laughter, which can make it hard to see. People pleasers are fun to be around, but in reality they laugh to keep from crying.

While people pleasers leave everyone else satisfied, they do not have the same sense of satisfaction in their lives. Perpetual people pleasers often kill their own dreams to satisfy others, and they can find themselves in a vicious cycle that leads to disappointment. How does a Tirzah break free? She must start by living to please God. In the last few decades, we asked ourselves, "What would Jesus do?" If you can relate to Tirzah, ask yourself, "What would Jesus have me do?" Although this may sound selfish, especially to those of us who were taught to consider others first, I am going to suggest something unthinkable: discover what *you're* meant to do. What do you like? What are you good at? These are often clues to your true calling.

Determine what God wants for you and begin to do that. You will never reach your potential in God if you only do what others want you to do. You must learn to prioritize your life and remember that God has given you value and a voice. You have the ability to create the life you desire, but you have to take your own God-directed steps to achieve it. Doing what everyone else wants or likes will not take you to the path that has been mapped out for your life.

I believe Tirzah made up her mind to be there with her sisters not because she wanted to please them but because she wanted what was rightfully hers. She had a stake in the action, so she took a courageous step to show up. She might have upset some of her friends and neighbors who thought she should just settle for the status quo, but she refused to live for them. Interestingly although that day in front of the Tent of Meeting wasn't a time for laughing, Tirzah's pleasant personality likely helped the elders hear the sisters' unified voice.

Perhaps you can relate to one of these sisters, or maybe you find a bit of yourself in all of them. Their personalities—their differences and similarities, their strengths and weaknesses—let us know they were not perfect women with perfect backgrounds. Each had character strengths and character flaws, and each could have allowed her personal circumstances to limit her, but none of them did. You may feel disadvantaged because you don't have the personality or skill set you desire. You may have even allowed this to limit your possibilities. But as we see in these sisters, the only real limits are the ones we place on ourselves.

STAND AND SPEAK UP

When the daughters of Zelophehad stood together to state their case and challenge the status quo, they made a mark on history. We sometimes marvel at those who do something so remarkable it is remembered generation after generation, but you don't have to be special to be a history maker. You don't have to be extraordinary to do something that changes someone's world. You just have to choose to take a step of faith and show up.

I am blessed to be born of two families with a rich legacy. On my father's side, my great-great-grandmother, Rachel Knight, was a mulatto former slave who was deeded land in the state of Mississippi. Her common-law husband, a white landowner named Newton Knight, ensured that she and their children would have an inheritance after his death. This was just after the Civil War, and the laws of Mississippi at that time were not written in their favor.

Rachel and Newton's marriage was not only illegal; it was also considered immoral. Although no woman of color had ever been deeded property up to that time, Newton and Rachel challenged the status quo when they walked into the courthouse in Jones County, Mississippi. Rachel received over 160 acres of land, which remains in the family today. Victoria Bynum documents their story in her book *The Free State of Jones*, which became a major motion picture in 2016.

On my maternal side, my great-aunt Anna Overton Glover became the first Negro woman in Austin, Texas, to be issued a driver's license. This was in the late 1940s.

Her husband had died, and she now was a single parent who didn't want to be dependent upon others to drive her and her young son where they needed to go. She also didn't want to be dependent upon public transportation, which was segregated at that time. My aunt Anna wanted a sense of independence that was a rarity among widows. In the late 1940s very few women embraced this kind of independence, and it was even rarer among women of color. No woman who looked like her or who lived in her neighborhood, or even in her city, had sought a driver's license. But on a sunny summer afternoon my aunt did the unthinkable and appeared before the Texas Department of Transportation to apply for her driver's license. Soon she was proudly driving through the city streets as a legal driver. I can imagine the heads that turned!

From both sides of my family I have learned powerful lessons. I've learned that I should never settle for something just because it's always been that way. And I've learned that sometimes *you have to challenge it to change it.* "It" is anything that limits me and keeps me living within a box. "It" is anything other than God that defines how far and how deep I can go. "It" is anything that makes me fearful of reaching beyond what everyone has said I am capable of doing. "It," I have come to realize, is the thing God wants me to keep in front of Him in my prayer life and to focus on as I grow in faith. The Bible says that with God all things are possible. Changing our "it" is possible when we live and walk with God. Breaking barriers is no easy task—it will take you and God working together to overcome your "it."

Inquire of the Lord

The Bible says Moses inquired of the Lord on the sisters' account. And God responded. Please know that whenever God is about to shift something in a major way, He will make His will clear.

When we are seeking to do big things in our lives, it is important that we seek God's direction before we make a move. Through prayer and supplication, with thanksgiving, we are told to make our requests known unto God (Phil. 4:6). We cannot depend only on our spiritual leaders to ask God for direction. Each of us must be responsible for our intercession and supplication. In other words, we have to ask God for help ourselves!

Moses was wise enough to inquire of the Lord when the sisters presented their case, and God spoke. There could be no challenge to the new order since it was not from Moses but rather from the Lord. Let's be real. There were people who did not want to see this change happen. I imagine many males in their clan— Zelophehad's uncles and cousins who stood to inherit the property without the girls' interference—were not happy about this. It meant they would receive less land. They could have challenged Moses's word, but not God's. The Bible says Moses inquired of the Lord and spoke what God said, which was "what Zelophehad's daughters are saying is right!" (Num. 27:7, NIV).

I think it is important that believers realize that the enemy always contests the promises of God. He doesn't want you to believe God's promises are for you because he doesn't want you to lay hold of them. Circumstances will make you think you cannot grasp the promise; situations will have you believing you are too far gone for God to release His promises to you. But that is not true. As author David Nicholas said, "God's promises are like the stars; the darker the night the brighter they shine."[10]

It isn't up to the devil whether we receive what God has for us. God's promises are yes and amen in Christ. The question is, Do we believe that? Satan's strategy is simple: he wants us to believe him instead of God and His Word. But the Bible says, "God is not a man, that He should lie, nor a son of man, that He should repent. Has He said, and will He not do? Or has He spoken, and will He not make it good?" (Num. 23:19, NKJV). Remember, "faith cometh by hearing, and hearing by the word of God" (Rom. 10:17, KJV). So if you want to walk in the promises of God, you'll need to drown out the enemy's lies and build up your faith by reminding yourself of what God says in His Word.

JUST ASK

The daughters of Zelophehad considered their circumstance, challenged it, and watched as God changed their destiny. These women shifted history and were able to claim a piece of the Promised Land! In Joshua 17 the women show up once again, but this time it wasn't to ask for their inheritance; it was to get what was promised to them!

One of the biggest challenges for Christians is to ask God for our desires and allow Him to fulfill them. He promises that if we delight ourselves in Him, He will give us the desires of our hearts (Ps. 37:4). Too often we settle for tradition or the status quo. We believe things are a certain way and nothing can be done to change them. But what if one person's voice could make a difference? Can you imagine living in that kind of world? Well, guess what? You do.

Maybe it's time for you to imagine *your* voice making a difference—to not only show up but also speak up. Had the daughters of Zelophehad not fought for their rights to receive property, no other women would have been able to receive land. But because of their courage their voices were heard, and it changed the trajectory for women in that day and allowed them to also possess the promise of God!

> Now Zelophehad son of Hepher, the son of Gilead, the son of Makir, the son of Manasseh, had no sons but only daughters, whose names were Mahlah, Noah, Hoglah, Milcah and Tirzah. They went to Eleazar the priest, Joshua son of Nun, and the leaders and said, "The LORD commanded Moses to give us an inheritance among our relatives." So Joshua gave them an inheritance along with the brothers of their father, according to the LORD's command.
> —JOSHUA 17:3–5, NIV

What had never been done before was no longer unthinkable; it became a reality. The sisters' preparedness and unity in approaching the leaders caused Moses to establish God-directed guidelines that blessed women for generations. Imagine if they had never taken that bold step to go before the elders uninvited and unannounced.

It was unthinkable that they would step forward. It was unthinkable that they would ask for property. And it was unthinkable that God would say yes! But to God, the unthinkable is often simply the unexplored. God can do anything, and it will always be greater than what we can imagine.

When I worked in corporate America, we were given an annual evaluation that impacted our sales bonuses and salary increases. It was our one opportunity to make a solid, documented impression upon management and to affect our salaries for the upcoming year. One year I showed up completely unprepared. I did not bring any documents of my sales, customer appreciation reports, or valuations, nor did I prepare a self-evaluation of my accomplishments that year.

Normally I would have prepared all of this in advance and walked in the room confident that my contributions to our team were sufficient to positively impact my salary. This year was different. Following the management style of my current boss, I had only marked highlights in my calendar showing how busy I had been, but no outcomes were documented. What I didn't realize was that a second manager would sit in on my evaluation and question every statement I made with a request for proof or documentation. My lack of preparation cost me five thousand dollars in bonuses and led to a much smaller salary increase than I was accustomed to receiving.

I learned a valuable lesson that day; show up, but show up prepared. After sulking for a day, I decided to ask the second manager if I could meet with him briefly.

I let him know that I wasn't looking for him to change his evaluation, but I wanted him to have a better understanding of my contribution to the success of our team. This time when I showed up, I was prepared and professional, as I should have been the first time. I was given a second chance to present myself and my work. That doesn't always happen in life. Not only was I blessed to be given this second chance, but the manager was so impressed that he changed his evaluation of my work, and I received both the salary increase and bonus I was expecting!

I often wonder what would have happened if I had not requested that second meeting. Although the money was important, it was more important to me that my company understood my value to our team. I couldn't allow a poor evaluation to define my work. I had to challenge that, and their impression and my outcome changed.

What about you? Where do you need to show up? What needs to be changed in your life? What have you been sensing God wants you to do that you've been too afraid to try? Philippians 4:6 tells us to "be anxious for nothing, but in everything by prayer and supplication, with thanksgiving, let your requests be made known to God" (NKJV). The Bible also says, "You do not have because you do not ask God" (James 4:2, NIV). Don't suffer in silence. Ask God to help! So what if you've never seen your "it" done before. God's playground is the area of impossibility. Don't accept "It's never been done" as the final answer. Don't accept "You're not capable" as the answer. Don't accept "You're too old or you don't have enough money or you aren't qualified" as the answer.

Show up prepared where God is leading you; challenge your "it"—and watch God change your life.

Do the Unthinkable

*Allow the Holy Spirit to Empower
You and Give You Courage*

> After this prayer, the meeting place shook, and they were all filled with the Holy Spirit. Then they preached the word of God with boldness.
> —Acts 4:31

Many people have asked me how I overcame fear and began to boldly speak the gospel of Christ. They wanted to know where the courage came from. In the beginning of my ministry I was extremely nervous about speaking in front of groups. My voice would shake as hard as my knees would. People often look surprised when I tell them it was the power of the Holy Spirit that gave me the courage and boldness I needed every time I stood up!

The Bible says in Acts 1:8 that we will receive power when the Holy Spirit comes upon us, and we will be His witnesses throughout the earth. When we accept Christ, we are filled with the Holy Spirit, who guides us into all truth and helps us live the Christian life. But we can also walk in the power of the Holy Spirit—that divine enablement that allows us to have uncommon wisdom, uncommon boldness, uncommon faith, and the like.

The apostle Paul wrote:

To one there is given through the Spirit a message of wisdom, to another a message of knowledge by means of the same Spirit, to another faith by the same Spirit, to another gifts of healing by that one Spirit, to another miraculous powers, to another prophecy, to another distinguishing between spirits, to another speaking in different kinds of tongues, and to still another the interpretation of tongues. All these are the work of one and the same Spirit, and he distributes them to each one, just as he determines.

—1 Corinthians 12:8–11, niv

God gave us the Holy Spirit to empower us uniquely to do what He has called us to do. I knew I was called to preach, so I prayed for God to give me the courage to accomplish His work, and He did! It was unthinkable that a nervous speaker would suddenly be bold, showing up in appropriate places, speaking His words. But God laughs at what we call impossible.

Do you need boldness and courage to do what God has called you to do? Today, ask God to fill you afresh with His Spirit. He will give you the boldness you need and equip you to walk in His power.

CHAPTER 4

UNTHINKABLE WISDOM
ABIGAIL

*David replied to Abigail, "Praise the Lord, the God
of Israel, who has sent you to meet me today! Thank
God for your good sense!... For I swear by the Lord,
the God of Israel, who has kept me from hurting you,
that if you had not hurried out to meet me, not one of
Nabal's men would still be alive tomorrow morning."*

—1 SAMUEL 25:32–34

H OW MANY TIMES have you heard the saying
"opposites attract"? Do you believe that, or do you
think it's just a catchphrase? I'm sure there is some truth
to it because several of my friends are married to men
whose personalities are the opposite of theirs. They say
their husbands' differences actually complement the

marriage and don't hurt it, and if they had to do it all over again, they would gladly marry the same man.

However, I have prayed with enough hurting couples to know that being married to someone who is very different can be challenging. Dr. Neil Warren, a clinical psychologist and founder of the popular online dating website *eHarmony*, encourages dating couples to proceed with caution if they have opposite characteristics. "I don't discount how hard it is to find someone who is a lot like you," he says. "It has always been difficult, and it's become even more so, as diversity increases. But when two people come from similar backgrounds, they operate from a position of strength. Their relationship is made significantly easier by all the customs and practices they have in common."[1]

What to look for in a potential husband isn't the main focus of this chapter, but it is the perfect segue to my next unthinkable character. Her name is Abigail. She was a beautiful woman whose wisdom saved her fool of a husband, Nabal, from certain death after he insulted David, who was later crowned king of Israel.

Yes, I called Nabal a fool, but you don't have to take my word for it. He and Abigail are introduced to us in 1 Samuel 25:1–3, where we learn a lot about them in just a few sentences:

> Then David moved down to the wilderness of Maon. There was a wealthy man from Maon who owned property near the town of Carmel. He had 3,000 sheep and 1,000 goats, and it was sheep-shearing time. This man's name was Nabal, and his wife, Abigail, was a sensible and beautiful

woman. But Nabal, a descendant of Caleb, was crude and mean in all his dealings.

From the moment we meet Nabal, we know he's trouble. He was wicked, foulmouthed, and mean-spirited. In fact, his name literally means "foolish" and "stupid."[2] Then out of nowhere Caleb is mentioned. When I first read "a descendant of Caleb," it seemed out of place to me. But after rereading about this great man of faith, I realized the text fit perfectly.

Nabal was able to build a lucrative sheep-shearing business because he owned prime property that had been passed down to him from his famous ancestor, Caleb, who had been among those who wandered in the wilderness after the great exodus from Egypt. When God told Moses to handpick twelve men to scout out the land of Canaan, Caleb was one of the spies. When he returned to Moses with a good report based on his faith in God and not fear, God rewarded him with the very land Nabal now possessed. Numbers 14:24 says: "But my servant Caleb has a different attitude than the others have. He has remained loyal to me, so I will bring him into the land he explored. His descendants will possess their full share of that land."

Nabal was the beneficiary of someone else's blessings, but his life is proof that godly character cannot be inherited. Abigail, however, is described as a sensible, beautiful woman with great understanding and a joyful spirit. Her name even means "cause of joy."[3] In this story it's clear that sometimes opposites don't attract; they distract!

ONE WAS WISE, ONE WAS FOOLISH

I don't know how Abigail became the wife of a fool. Perhaps her father agreed to give his beautiful daughter to Nabal in exchange for a handsome bride price. Whatever the case, I know that when she was confronted with a life-or-death situation, Abigail responded with a rare weapon: wisdom.

In 1 Samuel 25 David sent men to Nabal and kindly asked him for some food to feed his hungry troops. This was before David ascended the throne, when he was still dodging Saul's attempts to kill him. He and his men were living in the wilderness, moving from place to place.

Apparently, Nabal's servants had been tending their sheep near where David and his men had made camp, and David had been good to them. They didn't harass or steal from Nabal's servants; instead, they basically protected them. That is why David thought Nabal would be willing to offer his men some food.

> When David heard that Nabal was shearing his sheep, he sent ten of his young men to Carmel with this message for Nabal: "Peace and prosperity to you, your family, and everything you own! I am told that it is sheep-shearing time. While your shepherds stayed among us near Carmel, we never harmed them, and nothing was ever stolen from them. Ask your own men, and they will tell you this is true. So would you be kind to us, since we have come at a time of celebration? Please share

any provisions you might have on hand with us
and with your friend David."

—1 SAMUEL 25:4–8

Nabal's response was nothing like what David
expected. True to his name, Nabal was rude and
insulting to David's messengers.

"Who is this fellow David?" Nabal sneered to the
young men. "Who does this son of Jesse think he
is? There are lots of servants these days who run
away from their masters. Should I take my bread
and my water and my meat that I've slaughtered
for my shearers and give it to a band of outlaws
who come from who knows where?"

—1 SAMUEL 25:10–11

It's hard to imagine that anyone, especially a wealthy
landowner, one of Caleb's descendants, would be
unaware of David's exploits. At the very least he would
have known that David had killed the Philistine giant
Goliath. Some commentaries say Nabal knew very well
of David but that he had sided with the house of Saul
and shared the king's jealousy of David.[4] Yet one would
think a man would hesitate to make an enemy of a giant
killer when he's in his backyard. It would be a foolish
thing to do. But, of course, the Bible says Nabal was
a fool.

As soon as David heard what Nabal said, he grabbed
his sword and told his men to get theirs. With four hundred of his followers, David set out for Nabal's house
determined to leave no one alive by the next morning.

That is exactly what Nabal's servants thought David would do the moment they heard how Nabal responded to the future king. So they found Abigail and told her, "David sent messengers from the wilderness to greet our master, but he screamed insults at them. These men have been very good to us, and we never suffered any harm from them. Nothing was stolen from us the whole time they were with us. In fact, day and night they were like a wall of protection to us and the sheep. You need to know this and figure out what to do, for there is going to be trouble for our master and his whole family. He's so ill-tempered that no one can even talk to him!" (1 Sam. 25:14–17).

Just as they expected, Abigail immediately went into action.

> She quickly gathered 200 loaves of bread, two wineskins full of wine, five sheep that had been slaughtered, nearly a bushel of roasted grain, 100 clusters of raisins, and 200 fig cakes. She packed them on donkeys and said to her servants, "Go on ahead. I will follow you shortly." But she didn't tell her husband Nabal what she was doing.
>
> —1 SAMUEL 25:18–19

I believe every woman should read this story and take note of Abigail. Her story is so rich that she deserves her own book, but there are three big-picture truths I want to share in this chapter in hopes that we all will become more like her.

First, Abigail had godly wisdom. When she heard that David was going to kill Nabal for being condescending and disrespectful of him, she didn't go yelling and screaming at her husband. Had that been many women today, they would have told Nabal, "Because of your big mouth, every man in this family is going to die, including you!"

But Abigail must have known that it never pays to argue with a fool, because she did the opposite. She didn't even tell Nabal that she knew about all the ugly words he had spoken to David's messengers. Sometimes wisdom requires that we measure our words carefully and use them to calm a situation and not make matters worse.

I am blessed to be married to a man who does exhibit wisdom, but before I met him, I had been in relationships with people who made me feel vulnerable and insecure because they were constantly putting me in dangerous situations. I never knew what threat I might face from one moment to the next. One boyfriend was hotheaded and bad-tempered, and there were times when his anger was directed at me. Once I came close to being a victim of road rage when he began to pursue another driver who had been rude. After the other driver was out of sight, he turned his anger toward me because I tried to defuse the situation. I didn't want to defy him, but he was wrong—dead wrong. So to retaliate against me, he drove recklessly all the way back to his apartment. My heart was pounding hard in my chest because I was so afraid of what could have happened during the pursuit and while he was out of control.

Today I am grateful that even then God gave me wisdom beyond my years to be able to calm arguments and not make them worse. As a leader in ministry, I need wisdom. I can't live or lead without it. Don't think for minute that I haven't wanted to lash out at people who say mean things about me or the church behind my back and then grin in my face like we're best buddies. A wise, godly woman will pray before she responds.

In the case of the angry boyfriend, I prayed that level minds would prevail. God answered, and the guy and I were both able to walk away from what could have been a bad situation. If there is one prayer that I constantly keep before me, it is the one that hung on my mother's bedroom wall when I was a child: "God grant me the serenity to accept the things I cannot change; courage to change the things I can; and wisdom to know the difference." I can't tell you how many times the Serenity Prayer has helped me through a tough situation.

WE NEED THE HOLY SPIRIT

I don't know what Abigail prayed or if she prayed at all, but when she got the news about David, she prepared a peace offering. She gathered hundreds of pounds of food and gave the man of God what he requested, despite Nabal's selfishness.

The Bible says there are two types of wisdom, earthly and godly. Earthly wisdom is this: "But if you are bitterly jealous and there is selfish ambition in your heart, don't cover up the truth with boasting and lying. For jealousy and selfishness are not God's kind of wisdom" (James 3:14–15). The text goes on to say that where there is jealousy and selfish ambition, every evil imaginable is also there.

Now, juxtapose the definition of earthly wisdom with godly wisdom in James 3:17: "But the wisdom from above is first of all pure. It is also peace loving, gentle at all times, and willing to yield to others. It is full of mercy and the fruit of good deeds."

Do you know anyone who fits this description? I wish I could say that I have perfected all six of those qualities, but I'm a work in progress, as we all are. To have wisdom, though, we must first ask for it, and God will "generously" give it to us, according to James 1:5. This brings me to my next point: I believe it is impossible to live a lifestyle of godly wisdom without help from the Holy Spirit. The Spirit will tell us when and how to respond in every area of our lives. He is the Paraclete, the One who gives us counsel, and He is our *helper.* The Holy Spirit will prompt you if a response is needed, and He will let you know if nothing at all needs to be said or done.

For instance, my husband, who is excellent at many things but is not mechanically inclined, recently broke the garage door. He wasn't even sure how it happened. I didn't say a word about it even though I knew what had happened. He laughed with me about it later and said, "I remember a day when you would have fussed about that door, but this time you were really cool about it." That's because I had come to a place in life where I began to ask myself whether it was worth it to get myself all worked up. Would it have been worth it to argue about something that wasn't going to change? The answer is no, so I decided not to waste my energy yelling at him.

In a different situation God gave me the wisdom to know how to support my husband. As I began to recognize each of our strengths and weaknesses as leaders, I saw that I naturally enjoyed some of the tasks that he enjoyed the least. So I began to handle those tasks. Our complementary differences are what make us a great team. Wisdom has shown me that we don't need to compete; we each have unique contributions to make as leaders. Some couples who lead together, whether in ministry or business, find themselves butting heads or unable to agree on what approach or strategy is best. But this isn't what God desires. Wisdom can make all the difference!

EVERY WOMAN HAS A SECRET WEAPON

Earlier in the chapter I said that I would share three big-picture truths with you. The first is that Abigail had godly wisdom, which I just discussed. The second is that Abigail demonstrated humility—and it was actually wisdom that empowered her to walk in humility.

Humility means to have "a modest or low view of one's own importance."[5] And the Bible admonishes us to not think more highly of ourselves than we ought (Rom. 12:3). This is the opposite of how many people think they should be, but women who experience the unthinkable do the unexpected.

After Abigail prepared the food for David, she sent it on ahead and then set out toward his camp. Mind you, David was ready for battle, and Abigail had no weapons. Yet she disarmed him with her humility:

When Abigail saw David, she quickly got off her donkey and bowed low before him. She fell at his feet and said, "I accept all blame in this matter, my lord. Please listen to what I have to say. I know Nabal is a wicked and ill-tempered man; please don't pay any attention to him. He is a fool, just as his name suggests. But I never even saw the young men you sent.

"Now, my lord, as surely as the LORD lives and you yourself live, since the LORD has kept you from murdering and taking vengeance into your own hands, let all your enemies and those who try to harm you be as cursed as Nabal is. And here is a present that I, your servant, have brought to you and your young men. Please forgive me if I have offended you in any way. The LORD will surely reward you with a lasting dynasty, for you are fighting the LORD's battles. And you have not done wrong throughout your entire life.

Even when you are chased by those who seek to kill you, your life is safe in the care of the LORD your God, secure in his treasure pouch! But the lives of your enemies will disappear like stones shot from a sling!

"When the LORD has done all he promised and has made you leader of Israel, don't let this be a blemish on your record. Then your conscience won't have to bear the staggering burden of needless bloodshed and vengeance. And when the LORD has done these great things for you, please remember me, your servant!"

—1 SAMUEL 25:23–31

Wow, what an impassioned plea! Abigail not only assumed responsibility for the matter, but she interceded for her husband's life. Even though I'm sure Nabal had been mean and cruel to Abigail throughout their marriage, she still walked in love toward him. She could have encouraged David to take him out, but she didn't. Only the love of God can make you stand between life and death for someone, especially if the person seems to be unlovable.

I know some of you can relate to the way Abigail was likely treated. You know how it feels to be verbally abused, unappreciated, and subjected to all manner of issues in your marriage that have caused deep emotional pain. My prayer is that you would reach out to a licensed Christian marriage counselor in your state so you and your husband can get help for your relationship. The other thing I'd say is to turn your husband over to God in prayer. He knows what it will take to make him stop hurting you.

Another sentence that caught my attention in Abigail's plea is this line: "Now, my lord, as surely as the LORD lives and you yourself live, since the LORD has kept you from murdering and taking vengeance into your own hands, let all your enemies and those who try to harm you be as cursed as Nabal is" (1 Sam. 25:26).

Abigail knew God. You can tell by the way she spoke about Him to David that she had a relationship with Him. She knew enough about God to know that He hates murder. Yes, David was angry with Nabal for saying ugly words about him, but he had no right to take matters into his own hands by going after innocent men to kill them. The Word of the Lord says, "Vengeance is mine, I will repay" (Rom. 12:19, NKJV). Who knows what God would have done to punish David for slaughtering those men just to appease his own anger? It can be tempting, but getting even with someone who has hurt us is never acceptable.

No matter how high we climb the ladder of success, God wants to know that we will always remain humble. When I watch the news and I see that a high-powered individual has been exposed in a scandal, the person's downfall can usually be attributed to a lack of humility, whether or not the person knows it. It was Abigail's humility that kept David from sinning, and your humility can keep you from falling.

BEWARE OF THE P-WORD

Some people pretend to have humility, but more times than not their behavior is a masquerade for pride, which the dictionary says is "a feeling or deep pleasure or satisfaction derived from one's own achievements, the achievements of those with whom one is closely associated, or from qualities or possessions that are widely admired."[6]

Nabal was puffed up with pride. That's why he sneered when he told David's servant, "Who does this son of Jesse think he is?" Nabal knew that Samuel had anointed David king of Israel years earlier, even though David was currently on the run from Saul. But it must have given Nabal great pride to know that Israel's soon-to-be-king was at his mercy. This story should be a lesson to all of us that not only is pride dangerous, but it is also deadly, as we will soon find out.

It can be hard for a Christian to admit that he or she has a problem with pride. We can get so dressed up that we don't even recognize the sense of self-importance we have. But pride is so boastful that it cannot keep quiet. "*I* did this, and *I* did that." "*I* should be the worship leader because *I* have the better voice." "It wasn't until *I* prayed for her that she got healed." Watch out for the use of the personal pronoun *I*. It is usually one of the first signs of a prideful heart. But once again, thank God for the indwelling of the Holy Spirit. His role as helper is to convict us of that kind of high-minded thinking about ourselves and to bring us back into fellowship with God through repentance.

When Abigail came face-to-face with David, she got off her donkey, threw herself at his feet, and gave a heartfelt explanation of what had happened. She told him that she didn't even know about the men's request for food. And then she did what many Christians don't like to do: she asked David to forgive her if she had offended him. This is a huge problem among believers because Satan would like nothing more than to keep us riled up and angry, and then he uses pride to keep us from apologizing to one another. If you offend someone, be quick to say you're sorry. The uneasiness you feel (which is really conviction from the Holy Spirit) will go away once you apologize.

ABIGAIL IS HONORED

I thank God for the Abigails in the world. I am also grateful that I do not know many Nabals, though I realize men and women like him exist. Although we would rather not have any dealings with such people, they actually force us to do the unthinkable and push us toward our next level of service to the Lord. I wish there were another way, but painful situations and evil people force us to our knees for answers and strategies.

When Abigail heard that Nabal was going to lose his life to David, she didn't waste any time preparing two hundred loaves of bread, five sheep, nearly a bushel of grain, and one hundred clusters of raisins. The bread had already been baked, the sheep slaughtered, the grain roasted, and the raisins harvested. All she had to do was load the food on the donkey and go find David. Each day she had unknowingly been preparing for the biggest challenge of her life.

To accomplish the unthinkable, we must be prepared for whatever challenges come our way. How do we prepare? By praying, fasting, and reading the Word every day. That will equip us to put our faith into action. Thank God Abigail was prepared, because going before David to save Nabal's life was the unthinkable action that led her to her God-given purpose. What looked like an impossible situation was really preparation for something better.

> David replied to Abigail, "Praise the LORD, the God of Israel, who has sent you to meet me today!

Thank God for your good sense! Bless you for keeping me from murder and from carrying out vengeance with my own hands. For I swear by the LORD, the God of Israel, who has kept me from hurting you, that if you had not hurried out to meet me, not one of Nabal's men would still be alive tomorrow morning."

Then David accepted her present and told her, "Return home in peace. I have heard what you said. We will not kill your husband."

When Abigail arrived home, she found that Nabal was throwing a big party and was celebrating like a king. He was very drunk, so she didn't tell him anything about her meeting with David until dawn the next day. In the morning when Nabal was sober, his wife told him what had happened. As a result he had a stroke, and he lay paralyzed on his bed like a stone. About ten days later, the LORD struck him, and he died.

When David heard that Nabal was dead, he said, "Praise the LORD, who has avenged the insult I received from Nabal and has kept me from doing it myself. Nabal has received the punishment for his sin."

—1 SAMUEL 25:32–39

Nabal's death leads me to my third and final big-picture truth. Humility will always lead to honor. Proverbs 18:12 puts it this way: "Haughtiness goes before destruction; humility precedes honor." Another word for haughtiness is *pride*. Even though Nabal was proud, God gave him countless opportunities to change his wicked ways. Every morning that he woke up and saw his beautiful, humble wife, God was telling him to let go of the pride. It's the same message I feel God is speaking today. Let go of pride, be humble, walk in humility, and you will be honored for your obedience, just as Abigail was.

When Nabal died, David heard about it and sent his messengers to ask Abigail to marry him (1 Sam. 25:39–41). She had no idea that her wisdom and humility would lead to a marriage proposal from the future king of Israel. Her faith in God gave her the courage to risk her life for a fool, and she was rewarded for it. Notice that Abigail didn't ask God to kill her husband to free her of what was probably a miserable life. She simply walked in wisdom and humility, and God determined Nabal's fate as well as her own.

Abigail accepted David's proposal, and he made her his wife (1 Sam. 25:42). Not only did Abigail marry a man who shared her faith and love for God, but in time she also became a queen. Honor awaits the humble. Abigail is proof. Unthinkable wisdom—the wisdom that comes from above—brings unthinkable blessing.

DO THE UNTHINKABLE

Ask for Wisdom

If you need wisdom, ask our generous God, and he will give it to you.

—JAMES 1:5

I read once that wisdom comes with age. I wholeheartedly disagree with that statement, and I will admit to knowing some old fools. I think it is better to say that wisdom comes from God's allowing us to experience life and to get a clearer understanding of how to handle our experiences.

A wise person once told me that it's not enough to "have" wisdom if you aren't willing to "use" it. Let's be clear: wisdom comes with action—often unthinkable action. Place before God the situations that don't make sense or the ones that you do not know how to manage. The blessing of the unlimited wisdom of God can be yours if you just ask. Trust me, He will show you what to do!

CHAPTER 5

UNTHINKABLE BELIEF
RAHAB

"I know the Lord has given you this land," she told them.... "The Lord your God is the supreme God of the heavens above and the earth below."

—JOSHUA 2:9, 11

O N A TYPICAL night she could expect a knock on the door, and her business depended on the consistency of that knock. Somehow, without a marketing plan or a promotional package, word of her business had spread. She was good, her merchandise was good, and most importantly Rahab knew how to keep a secret. So when a knock came that night, it seemed like business as usual. As usual there was a man at the door—two, in fact. But the moment she saw them, Rahab knew these men were not her typical clientele.

It was obvious they weren't from Jericho, but there was more to it than that. They were Israelites, the people who had spawned all the rumors. She'd heard the stories—that their God had delivered them from bondage in Egypt, parted the Red Sea so they could walk across on dry ground, and caused them to defeat the mighty Amorite kings Og and Sihon. She knew the people of Jericho were afraid of the Israelites and their God, but the men at her door didn't frighten her. If anything, they piqued her curiosity.

She opened the door to let the Israelites inside, and I imagine a rather awkward conversation ensued. They weren't looking for what she normally had to offer. They just wanted a place to stay for the night. Yes, Rahab had rooms, but she was more than an innkeeper, as some would suggest. Zanah, the Hebrew word used to describe her line of work, indicates that she was, in fact, a prostitute.[1]

There were many types of prostitutes in her day, including those who served in the temples of the Canaanite gods, but Rahab was just an ordinary girl, though by all accounts a successful one. Her house was in a great location near the city wall, perhaps even near the entry gate, and she dried stalks of flax on her rooftop that could be used for weaving linens and rope. Rahab seems like the kind of woman who learned early on to use what she had to get ahead.

Though great for business, the location of Rahab's establishment spelled trouble for the Israelites. Built against the town wall, the house had a stairway leading up to the roof that seemed to be a continuation of the wall. This meant everyone could see who went in and out.[2] With word spreading about Israel's exploits, she knew these men weren't safe. Someone would have seen them, and someone would be coming to her door before long.

"This way," I imagine Rahab said as she led the men to the roof. Moving the stalks of flax aside, she told them to hide. "The king will hear you came here. There's no way for you to have been missed. Just stay here. I'll take care of them."

Scripture seems to suggest messengers from the king were soon at her door, wanting her to hand over the men. They were Hebrew spies, after all, sent to search out the city. To protect them was treason, but to hand them over must have felt like a type of treason too. Rahab might not have been able to explain it, but I imagine she felt strangely drawn to these men from Israel. So rather than give them up, Rahab did the unthinkable. She lied to the king's men.

> Yes, the men were here earlier, but I didn't know where they were from. They left the town at dusk, as the gates were about to close. I don't know where they went. If you hurry, you can probably catch up with them.
> —JOSHUA 2:4–5

What could have possessed Rahab to assist the spies? Treason was punishable by death. Why would she risk her life to help total strangers? She was a Canaanite.

What was she doing helping the very people everyone feared would attempt to conquer their city? Even if she didn't care about her own life, didn't she care about her people? It was unthinkable.

Rahab's motive would soon become clear. When the king's men were gone, Rahab went up to the roof. She wanted to talk to the spies, to tell them what she had been thinking ever since they walked into her house.

> "I know the LORD has given you this land," she told them. "We are all afraid of you. Everyone in the land is living in terror. For we have heard how the LORD made a dry path for you through the Red Sea when you left Egypt. And we know what you did to Sihon and Og, the two Amorite kings east of the Jordan River, whose people you completely destroyed. No wonder our hearts have melted in fear! No one has the courage to fight after hearing such things. For the LORD your God is the supreme God of the heavens above and the earth below."
>
> —JOSHUA 2:9–11

Assuming Rahab had been taught the religion of Canaan, she might have surprised herself with the words she spoke that night: "the LORD your God is the supreme God of the heavens above and the earth below" (Josh. 2:11).

Like her family, she likely had been raised to worship Baal. An agrarian people, the Canaanites believed Baal, the god that controlled the rains, was the key to a good harvest.[3] So they did their best to appease him, lest they all starve.

Yet here was Rahab, bucking what she had known and declaring the God of Israel to be "the supreme God of the heavens above and the earth below." That means she was declaring Him to be higher and more powerful than the gods she had known her entire life. She didn't say that just to flatter the Hebrew visitors or to protect herself. Nor was she simply repeating what she had heard others say in secret. Rahab's words were a declaration of faith.

Fear had gripped all of Jericho, but the fear that filled Rahab was a reverential fear. That holy fear forced her to reassess what she believed, and when she did, she came to a new conclusion. She'd never heard of the Canaanite gods doing any of the things the Israelites' God had done. If the God of Israel could do such mighty things, she reasoned, He must be supreme.

On the rooftop with the spies Rahab put her newfound faith into action. The God of Israel was big and powerful, and He would conquer Jericho, but she wanted to live. And she wanted her family to live. So, ever the businesswoman, she brokered a deal.

> "Now swear to me by the LORD that you will be kind to me and my family since I have helped you. Give me some guarantee that when Jericho is conquered, you will let me live, along with my father and mother, my brothers and sisters, and all their families."
>
> "We offer our own lives as a guarantee for your safety," the men agreed. "If you don't betray us, we

will keep our promise and be kind to you when
the LORD gives us the land."

—JOSHUA 2:12–14

You may know the rest of the story. Rahab helped the spies escape by extending a rope down the side of her house. She told them to run to the hill country and hide there for three days, then go on their way. The spies, in turn, told her to leave the scarlet rope hanging from the same window when the Israelites came into the land. If all of her relatives were in her house when Israel took Jericho, they would be spared. But they wouldn't promise that anyone outside her house would be protected.

The spies did as she instructed, and they made it back to their camp safely. Rahab too followed the spies' directives, and she and her family were saved. Rahab's unthinkable belief secured a future for her and her family—and it changed the course of her life.

BREAKING THE MOLD

There are only two women mentioned in the "Hall of Faith" in Hebrews 11, and Rahab is one of them. Despite her background and occupation, God used Rahab as an integral part of His plan to bring His people to the land of promise. Rahab's assistance was key to the Israelites' success. So how did a woman once known for her sins become famous for her faith?

Indeed, Rahab's decision to follow the God of Israel was an unlikely one. She had spent her entire life as part of a culture that refused to accept the God of Israel. She hadn't witnessed the mighty acts God performed in the wilderness. She hadn't seen Him deliver the Israelites out of slavery in Egypt. To our knowledge, she hadn't been told of how God promised to make Abraham's descendants into a great nation even though he and his wife were childless. Yet, with the odds stacked against her, Rahab believed.

The Bible says in Romans 10:17 that "faith comes by hearing, and hearing by the word of God" (NKJV). Rahab heard again and again about the exploits of the God of Israel, and at some point her confidence shifted. When she went up to the rooftop to talk to the spies, she told them, "*I know* the LORD has given you this land" (Josh. 2:9, emphasis added). She was convinced that God would get the victory in Jericho, just as He had won the victory so many times before.

When Rahab heard what God could do, she believed He would do it again. I wish more Christians had that kind of confidence. So often people hear of the amazing things God has done for others—that He restored marriages, brought wayward children back home, healed diseases, blessed infertile couples with children, and brought hope to those in despair. But they don't believe He will do the same for them when they're sick or when their marriage is in trouble. That's not the kind of faith we see in Rahab. She believed God would do what He'd done before once again.

You may wonder how a bunch of stories of Israel's conquests could lead Rahab to trust God and His representatives, the spies, so completely. What was so convincing that she was willing to abandon the faith and the people she had known her entire life and align herself with these foreigners? We do not know everything Rahab was privy to hear, and we don't know if she took steps to verify the things she had been told. But personally I don't think Rahab had to conduct a bunch of research to be convinced the stories she'd heard were true. I believe what Rahab had heard about God only confirmed what she felt in her spirit.

Some people make their decisions about God after careful study, dotting every *i* and crossing every *t* until they are convinced that God must be real. Others encounter God supernaturally and become convinced that what they've read in the Bible is true. Rahab didn't have long to study God. She didn't have long to compare the gods of Canaan with the God of Israel. Nor did she have experiences to weigh her knowledge against. All she had were rumors about what God had done. When the Israelite spies were in her home and the king's messengers were at her door, she had to make a split-second decision, so she chose to trust what she sensed was right.

Something inside her knew not to hand over the spies. Something inside her knew the God of Israel was the true God. I believe that "something" was divine intuition. Frequently I hear people say that you cannot trust your intuition. And it is true that we should trust God's Word and the leading of His Spirit over a gut feeling. But I'd never want anyone to ignore that nagging feeling in her gut. When our knowledge of God or our sense of what He would want us to do is limited, I believe the Holy Spirit will use those "gut feelings" to guide us in the direction He wants us to go.

I believe that's what happened with Rahab. She didn't know much about God at that time in her life, but she had been given intuition from above that the spies were men of God.[4] So when she had seconds to make a decision—open the door and let them discover the spies, or open the door and misdirect the king's men so the spies could escape—she knew which path to take.

Interestingly to help the men escape, Rahab lied about the spies' whereabouts. The fact that God used Rahab's lie to accomplish His purposes for her and the Israelites is a mystery of His sovereignty; it doesn't make lying OK. Perhaps it was because Rahab lied that the spies weren't certain they could trust her. It may be why they told her, "If you don't betray us, we will keep our promise and be kind to you when the Lord gives us the land" (Josh. 2:14). While it wasn't right for Rahab to lie, the Bible commends her faith, which is what motivated her to act.

Our Beliefs Determine Our Destiny

Rahab didn't stop with her profession of faith. She backed up her statement with action. The plain-and-simple fact of life is this: our beliefs determine our behavior, and our behavior determines our outcomes. What Rahab believed determined how she acted, and her actions caused her life to be spared.

It is important to realize how our deeply rooted beliefs can impact how we react to a situation. Some beliefs serve us well; others limit us. When a belief is affirmed by experience, it can seem like a fact of life. In reality sometimes our beliefs are rooted in falsities that others claim as truths. Have you ever been in a situation where things didn't turn out at all as you thought they would? I sure have, and sadly more often than I would like.

When I asked myself why I believed the situation would turn out a certain way, I realized it was because of what someone told me. We often get confounded by others' beliefs and never move beyond those boundaries to know the truth for ourselves. This is how we become limited individuals who end up living within the confines of our own fears, distrust, and biases. I finally realized that trusting someone else's limited experience instead of seeking the truth for myself limited my world. I had to change my thinking to expand my horizons, and that changed my life!

We all have been impacted at some time in life by mistaken beliefs. As impressionable children, we receive messages from those in authority over us—parents, teachers, and other adults—and we take in these messages and make them part of our belief system. These messages impact our lives in a major way, whether good or bad. For instance, if a child is told she can accomplish whatever God leads her to do, those words will shape her beliefs about herself and her abilities. But if a child is told she will never amount to anything, she may believe that is true and allow those words to become a self-fulfilling prophecy.

When negative messages repeatedly infiltrate a person's psyche, the individual can become apathetic about life and think, "Why even try if I am going to fail?" Maybe you have spoken those very words yourself. If so, perhaps you need to question what you believe. Why do you believe you're going to fail? If you take the time to really think about it, chances are you will begin to remember the negative statements you have absorbed into your belief system.

Challenge those beliefs by declaring the truth. Jesus said in John 17:17 that God's Word is truth. So instead of believing the lies others have spoken to you, reshape your thinking by reminding yourself of how God sees you. Tell yourself:

- "I am fearfully and wonderfully made" (Ps. 139:14).

- "I am forgiven" (Col. 1:14).

- "I am precious to God" (Isa. 43:4).

- "I am more than a conqueror through Christ" (Rom. 8:37).

- "I am loved dearly by God" (John 15:13; 16:27; Rom. 5:8; Eph. 3:17-19).

- "I am valuable (1 Cor. 6:20).

- "I have a sound mind" (2 Tim. 1:7).

- "I am significant" (John 15:5).

- "I have been chosen by God to bear fruit" (John 15:16).

- "I can do all things through Christ who strengthens me" (Phil. 4:13).[5]

- "I am strong in the Lord and in the power of His might" (Eph. 6:10).

Negative words have power over you only because you treat them as the truth. In 2 Corinthians 10:5 the Bible says we are to "demolish arguments and every pretension that sets itself up against the knowledge of God, and…take captive every thought to make it obedient to Christ" (NIV). This means we must reject thoughts that are not in line with God's plan. Search the Scriptures to discover what God says about whatever negative message you have received, and then declare the truth over yourself, even if it feels weird. The more you remind yourself of the truth, the more your thinking will change. It's time for the negative thinking and self-fulfilling limitations to come to an end. Change the way you think, and you will change your life.

Can you imagine how much baggage Rahab had to release? Even after she changed her life, Scripture repeatedly refers to her as "the harlot Rahab" (Josh. 6:17; Heb. 11:31; James 2:25). But Rahab knew who she truly was. She knew what God had done for her and that she was not the person she had been. And that belief—not what others said about her—affected her behavior.

Beliefs shape behavior.

Our belief systems cause us to act and to respond a certain way. As stated earlier, belief systems serve as guidelines to our actions. In many ways they also provide boundaries for how we live. Some of our behavior is learned; some of it is a result of our personalities. Take, for example, a sporting event. We cheer our teams forward to victory, applauding the good they do. However, when the opposing team or officials seem to impede our team's progress, we show our disapproval with sighs, boos, thumbs down, and an occasional, "Ref, are you blind?"

We learn this behavior by watching others around us respond in this manner. Our belief system is that our cheers and verbal affirmations will help our preferred team win the game, and those who impede that win deserve to hear our displeasure. As someone whose son played sports as a child, I must admit how embarrassed I am by the way I sometimes behaved at my son's games. My belief that our team was the best and deserved to win caused me to look for a reason for each loss, and I usually determined that it was the lack of skill or fairness of the officials calling the game. Fortunately I would never discourage the children on the other team, but I was certainly not above blaming a loss on the referees. My beliefs led to my behavior.

After Rahab declared that the God of Israel was "the supreme God of the heavens above and the earth below," we read no accounts of her soliciting new clients or continuing her previous line of work. In fact, we see her helping the Israelites. Her newfound beliefs caused Rahab to behave differently, and her behavior led to a specific outcome.

Behavior shapes outcomes.

Rahab took several specific actions based on her belief that the God of Israel was the true God. First, she let the spies inside her house. That wasn't entirely unusual since the nature of her business would cause her to open her doors to many strangers. But second, she hid the spies before the king's men arrived. Whether they asked to be hidden or she recognized their need to take cover, the Israelites were on the roof covered with stalks of flax before the king's messengers arrived. Third, she redirected the king's search party and sent them the wrong way, after which she went to the roof and shared her new beliefs with the spies and asked for salvation.

Last, she stayed true to her word and helped the spies escape the city, then followed their instructions to a tee. To ensure her family was safe when the Israelites attacked, she gathered everyone in her home and placed the scarlet cord in her window so she and her family would be spared. Her new beliefs caused her to do all of this.

When we read the story of Rahab, it's easy to miss all the actions she took after she professed her faith in the God of Israel. Rahab didn't just talk about believing in God; she put her faith into action!

I am reminded of the words of James:

> What does it profit, my brethren, if someone says he has faith but does not have works? Can faith save him?...Likewise, was not Rahab the harlot also justified by works when she received the messengers and sent them out another way? For as the body without the spirit is dead, so faith without works is dead also.
> —JAMES 2:14, 25–26, NKJV

Rahab came a long way from her past. Her newfound belief didn't erase what she had done, but it gave her an opportunity to start anew. As I mentioned, she is one of only two women mentioned in Hebrews 11's Hall of Faith, and she is referenced in James as a person whose faith coupled with works led to salvation. Although those remembrances are powerful, the most amazing mention of Rahab, to me, is the one time she is spoken of without a reference to her former occupation.

In the Matthew 1 genealogy of Jesus, there is a woman named along with Abraham, Isaac, and David. She is listed simply as Rahab. But we know it is her—the same woman who was a harlot, the same Rahab who hid the spies in her home, the same Rahab who professed faith in a God she had not been raised to serve, the same Rahab who sought salvation for herself and her family. Yes, the Rahab with the scarlet cord—I am sure it is her.

Not much of her new life is written of in the Old Testament, only that she was the mother of Boaz. But this is remarkable since Boaz became the husband of Ruth, and they became parents to Jesse, who was the father of David, who became Israel's great king. Could it be that after the fall of Jericho and the integration of Rahab and her family into the Israelite community, this woman led a normal life, becoming a wife and a mother? Could it be that because of her faith in their God, she was accepted into a community of people who had been instructed not to intermarry with foreigners?

You may ask yourself how a woman who was a foreigner, a prostitute, and an idol worshipper could become the wife and mother of men who were deeply respected by their community. How could her life change so radically that she became the great-great-grandmother of a king? I suppose it's because her belief system shifted, and she chose to follow a new path. When she declared her faith out loud, her destiny changed, as her behavior followed her belief.

Do the Unthinkable

Choose to Believe

"I do believe, but help me overcome my unbelief!"
—Mark 9:24

Sitting in the doctor's office with my mother, I remember listening as her physician read the clinical report and gave her the diagnosis: Alzheimer's disease. Mom argued with her, "No, no, no. There is no way I'm going to lose all of my memories and forget who my children are!" She looked her in the eyes and said, "I know you believe what you see, but my God has the final say about my life. I *am* a believer."

As I watched the exchange, I felt so weak. I believed God was able to do the miraculous, but part of me thought, "This is going to happen just as the doctor said. Mom will forget who we are." Suddenly I felt myself being shaken. Mom was looking at me, asking, "What do you believe?" I couldn't deny the medical evidence, so all I could say was, "Lord, help my unbelief."

Faced with the terrible diagnosis of Alzheimer's disease, which affects a person's memory, behavior, and thinking, my siblings and I were all without words. Sadly as the disease progresses, many patients lose memories and their ability to carry on conversations. My mother lived with that diagnosis for six years before her body succumbed to its devastating effects. In time her communication with us became severely limited, but she never forgot who we were.

Every time my sister, brother, husband, children, or I walked into the room, she called us by name until she stopped speaking. She never forgot us. God did have the final say. She believed He would keep her, and He did.

As you face your own challenges and fears, you too must ask yourself, "What do I believe?" Our God is limitless in His mercy and grace toward us. If you need an unthinkable measure of belief, ask Him for it today.

CHAPTER 6

UNTHINKABLE COMMITMENT
RUTH

*Where you go I will go, and where you stay I will
stay. Your people will be my people and your God
my God....May the LORD deal with me, be it ever
so severely, if even death separates you and me.*

—RUTH 1:16–18, NIV

W HEN YOU THINK of your mother-in-law or your
daughter-in-law, what's the first thought that
comes to mind? Do you respect her and shower her with
love and kindness, or does the very mention of her name
make you shudder? Whether or not you have in-laws,
do not skip this chapter. You're going to read about the
most renowned daughter-in-law in Scripture.

If you value integrity and want a model for how to serve God above fleshly desires, this woman is one for comparison. If you want a model for how to live your life motivated by faith and not fear, her story has something to teach you. If you want a model for how following God's plan for your life can make you bolder than you could ever be on your own and lead you to greater things than you could ever imagine for your life, then look closely at the choices this woman made.

This woman was unaware of the important role she would play in history, but the omniscient God of Israel knew. He made certain she was born into the right family, lived in the right city, and married the right man so she would meet the woman who became her mother-in-law. The two developed an unbreakable bond that was critical to each woman's fulfilling her God-given purpose. When women bond together in Christian unity—whether as sisters, colleagues, mothers and daughters, or in-laws—a supernatural exchange occurs. God gives us wisdom, favor, and divine strategy, and before we know it, the unthinkable happens!

Such was the case in the life of Ruth. Her story is one of heartbreak for certain, but there is also no denying that she played a central role in God's divine plan to bring Jesus into the world despite her nation of origin. Her story unfolds in the book of the Bible that bears her name.

Because of a famine in the land, a man named Elimelek moved from Bethlehem in Judah to the country of Moab with his wife, Naomi, and their sons, Mahlon and Kilion. After a while Elimelek died, and Naomi had only her two sons. The boys married Moabite women, one named Orpah and the other named Ruth, and they began building a life in Moab. But after they had been in Moab for about ten years, Naomi's sons also died. I know it sounds like a tragedy, but hang on. The story is just beginning.

Naomi heard that the Lord had shown grace to His people and provided food for them in Bethlehem. So the Bible says, "With her two daughters-in-law she left the place where she had been living and set out on the road that would take them back to the land of Judah" (Ruth 1:7, NIV).

YOUR PEOPLE WILL BE MY PEOPLE

The news that God had provided food was a sign to Naomi that it was time to return home. Naomi was an Israelite, so she surely grew up hearing about the faithfulness of God and the many awesome miracles He had performed for her people. He miraculously parted the Red Sea so her ancestors could escape Pharaoh's army during their exodus from Egypt. He sent manna from heaven to feed those same ancestors when they complained that there was no food to eat. And He supernaturally protected the Israelites from their enemies during their journey to the Promised Land. Unbeknownst to Naomi, the same God who led her ancestors through the wilderness was leading her back to Judah.

The three women set out together for Bethlehem, but at some point during their travels Naomi told her daughters-in-law to return to Moab. Ruth and Orpah were devastated. You could hear the sadness in their voices when she told them to leave.

"Go back, each of you, to your mother's home," Naomi lovingly, but firmly, insisted. "May the LORD show you kindness, as you have shown kindness to your dead husbands and to me. May the LORD grant that each of you will find rest in the home of another husband" (Ruth 1:8–9, NIV). She then kissed the women good-bye and planned to continue on her journey, but Ruth and Orpah cried aloud in protest: "We will go back with you to your people" (Ruth 1:10, NIV).

But Naomi was emphatic. "Why would you come with me? Am I going to have any more sons, who could become your husbands? Even if I thought there was still hope for me—even if I had a husband tonight and then gave birth to sons—would you wait until they grew up? Would you remain unmarried for them? No, my daughters. It is more bitter for me than for you, because the LORD's hand has turned against me!" (Ruth 1:11–13, NIV).

The women continued to argue with Naomi, but eventually she convinced Orpah to return to her mother's house and her gods in Moab. But Ruth would not be swayed. "Don't urge me to leave you or to turn back from you," Ruth pleaded. "Where you go I will go, and where you stay I will stay. Your people will be my people and your God my God. Where you die I will die, and there I will be buried. May the LORD deal with me, be it ever so severely, if even death separates you and me" (Ruth 1:16–17, NIV).

Ruth's response is one of the most endearing passages I have ever read in the Bible. She could have lashed out at Naomi and insisted that she was too old to know what was in her own best interest. But she did no such thing.

I believe Ruth's words were an impromptu reaction to the sacrificial love and respect God had put in her heart. Ruth's willingness to follow Naomi to the grave, literally, was nothing short of supernatural.

It's Not Where We Come From That Matters Most

We humans are innately sinful, incapable of loving one another without the love of God already abiding in us. Love is what motivated Jesus to take our place on the cross and die for our sins. This means doing the unthinkable has nothing to do with how good we are or how perfect we are not. We become women who do the unthinkable by knowing Jesus Christ as our Lord and Savior, repenting of our sins, and inviting Him to live in our hearts, which brings me to Orpah.

Many preachers have scandalized her name because she returned to her mother's house in Moab. It wasn't that Orpah didn't deeply care about her mother-in-law. We can tell she did because Naomi told her, "May the LORD show you kindness, as you have shown kindness to your dead husbands and to me" (Ruth 1:8). Orpah was also willing to follow her mother-in-law. We know that because when it was time to leave Moab she followed Naomi of her own free will. I believe the tragedy of Orpah's story is not that she didn't love Naomi; it's that she did not love God.

First John 2:15 warns us to "love not the world, neither the things that are in the world. If any man love the world, the love of the Father is not in him" (KJV). Moab was a worldly place known for its many pagan gods. It was named for a man named Moab, who was a descendant of Lot, Abraham's nephew (Gen. 12:5). Moab was conceived in incest when Lot's oldest daughter got her father drunk so she could sleep with him and become pregnant (Gen. 19:30–37).

Moab's descendants, the Moabites, sacrificed their precious children on the fiery altars of the god Chemosh and performed many other godless rituals such as temple prostitution.[1] The land of Moab had become the kind of place that typifies the fact that when the truth of God's love is not in us, it's easy to become immersed in sin.

However, despite the moral corruption in Moab, where Ruth was born, God chose this woman with incest in her ancestral bloodline to do His will. Ruth was not an Israelite. She was not a Jew. Yet her story is important enough to be included in Scripture. Why? It's because Ruth exemplifies the truth that with God it doesn't matter where we come from or the sins in our past. He will use us regardless of our history to do unthinkable exploits for Him if we accept the grace of salvation He offers us.

It is hard to deny the truth when God plants it inside us. Ruth could see the truth, a truth that liberated her from the same pagan worship Orpah enjoyed. That is why she knew that going with her mother-in-law was the right choice for her, the right path for her life. There aren't many people who know what it's like to come from a completely pagan land, be introduced to God through marriage, and then be faced with the decision to go back to the pagan life they once knew or move forward into the unknown.

Ruth did not know that she was speaking prophetically about the role she would play in the birth of Jesus Christ when she told Naomi, "Your people will be my people." Had Ruth returned to Moab with Orpah, she would have forfeited her divine purpose. The only real option in Ruth's heart was to bravely move forward into what God had waiting for her because she had a new nature that no longer fit in Moab.

Whatever you do, don't be like Orpah and return to the old nature. She is proof that it's not enough for us to get out of Moab; we must also get the spirit of Moab out of us! First, you have to repent of your sins and ask Jesus to come into your heart and save you. Second, saturate your heart and mind with the Word of God so you'll have the mind of Christ and hear His voice. Romans 12:2 says, "And be not conformed to this world: but be ye transformed by the renewing of your mind" (KJV). Finally, get ready to surrender to the Holy Spirit. He's going to help you resist the Moab mind-set and empower you to live a holy life so you can do the unthinkable, the way Ruth did when she followed Naomi.

COURAGE AND FRIENDSHIP

Most of us would have run from a situation like the one Ruth faced. But here's part of the reason she didn't run: Ruth was so connected to Naomi, she felt that staying with her was part of her life's calling, that God had put her in a position to help Naomi release her bitterness.

How ironic that Naomi, whose name means "pleasant-ness,"[2] told her daughters-in-law that life was bitter for her. Naomi was bitter because the people she loved the most had died. She thought their deaths were a sign that God's hand was against her.

We don't like it, but suffering serves a very valuable purpose in our lives. We grow the most in our faith when we go through tests and trials because pain forces us to surrender our will to God. I often wonder if Ruth learned to trust God when everything in her life was going well or if she built her spiritual muscle by exercising her faith in God after her husband, Mahlon, died. Mahlon's name means "sick."[3] It's possible that he was a sickly person most of his life and died due to his frailty. But even if Mahlon had been ill, his passing would have been extremely painful for Ruth and Naomi.

It's easy to praise God and obey His every word when we have everything we think we need. But what happens when it all falls apart? What happens when your fifty-year-old husband announces that he's leaving you for a woman twenty years his junior, or when your child is diagnosed with an incurable disease and given only months to live? Such problems are enough to make a person curse God, the way Job's wife suggested he do in Job 2:9.

But Ruth didn't choose that path. I believe her suffering deepened her trust in the Lord, clarified her convictions, and honed her character. That's why she had the courage to leave her mother, father, sisters, and brothers, if she had any, for a life with Naomi. God had done an obvious work in her heart, healing her from the pain of her husband's death. Her name means "friend-ship,"[4] so it's clear that God was also using this close friendship to transform Naomi's bitterness.

There is speculation among theologians as to exactly how long Naomi lived in Moab before she returned to her homeland. Ruth 1:4 says it "was about ten years." It was a thirty-mile journey back to Bethlehem from Moab, and when Ruth and Naomi entered the city days later, the women there were all abuzz about Naomi's returning home. Naomi didn't know it, but the timing of her arrival, at the beginning of barley season (Ruth 1:22), had been perfectly orchestrated by God.

But Naomi didn't see God's plan at work. This is why when the women in Bethlehem greeted her, she said:

> "Don't call me Naomi.... Call me Mara, because the Almighty has made my life very bitter. I went away full, but the LORD has brought me back empty. Why call me Naomi? The LORD has afflicted me; the Almighty has brought misfortune upon me."
> —RUTH 1:19–21, NIV

Have you ever been so hurt by circumstances that you told anybody who would listen that God was to blame? It's easy to blame Him for everything that goes wrong in our lives, especially since He's all powerful and could easily make the hurt go away. You think God must be angry with you or that He doesn't care about you, because if He did, surely He would stop the bleeding. These thoughts seem logical when we can't figure out how to stop the pain, but they're not true. We should rebuke Satan in Jesus's name every time he opens his mouth to make these kinds of accusations. God will never, ever forsake us. Psalm 34:19 says, "Many are the afflictions of the righteous, but the LORD delivers him out of them all" (NKJV).

Naomi's deliverance was already in the works, but it was Ruth's willingness to follow her mother-in-law's instructions that later brought blessing to both women beyond anything they could have dreamed. That's because Naomi and Ruth had what I believe was the perfect mentoring relationship. Mentoring is critically important to the body of Christ because learning and gaining godly wisdom from someone who is more spiritually mature can empower the mentee to be more effective in every area of her life—at home, at church, and at work.

People today say they want a mentor, but they often aren't prepared to sacrifice the time and energy needed to build a strong relationship. What some really want is to be connected to somebody who has ascended higher on the ladder of success and who can pull them up to a better position. That's not mentoring. To mentor someone is to teach and "give guidance" to someone who is typically younger, whether in age or in life experiences.[5]

SEARCHING FOR AN IDENTITY

Mentoring has always played a major role in my life, especially in my early days in ministry. I have a bachelor's degree in biology and chemistry, and my education opened the door for me to move up the corporate ladder and establish myself in pharmaceutical sales. At one point during my career I took a huge leap of faith and accepted a different position as a trainer making a six-figure salary with bonuses every year.

In 1999, however, I resigned from my great corporate job. I had already begun to feel God's tugging on my heart to begin working for the church when my employer announced its third merger in two years. After the merger I learned my position would be based in a city four hours away by car and that I would have to be in that office three days each workweek. I knew the time away from home would be too much for my family, especially since my sons were in elementary school at the time.

After I resigned, I had what I call an identity crisis. I was a housewife, a preacher's wife, and a volunteer, but I had become unsure of myself because I went from being a confident career woman earning a great salary to not knowing what I was supposed to be doing or even how to discover that answer.

In 2002 I went into full-time vocational ministry at the church. I was the director of ministries, overseeing the lay ministries, with my husband as the senior pastor. But eventually I began to lead in a broader capacity, and I started to preach. When that happened, I knew I had to have a huge paradigm shift because professionally I wasn't what I used to be, yet I didn't know what I was supposed to be. I grew up in a very traditional Baptist church where the roles for women were definitely limited—which meant women were not allowed to preach. I remember one time when my grandfather, who was the pastor of the church, took issue with a woman who had stood up and said God called her to preach. Why did she say that? My grandfather wrestled the microphone from her, pushed her down in the chair, and said: "God doesn't call women to preach. Go back and hear God!" And with that I was taught that women were to have constrained roles in the church.

It was a challenging time for me, but thank God for the women who became my mentors and gave me the guidance and encouragement I needed. They were powerful examples of women who were succeeding in the very same roles God was calling me to. I sought out events and conferences that could prepare me for the position that God had defined and for the elevation He was giving me. I was able to grow personally and spiritually from the instruction and wisdom I received from women I call "the Big Girls" of female preachers. They are the Reverend Cynthia Hale, the Reverend Claudette Copeland, the Reverend Jessica Ingram, the Reverend Elaine Flake, and the Reverend Carolyn Showell, who were all co-conveners of the Women in Ministry Conference. As a group, whether up close or from afar, they taught me the value of my calling as a woman in ministry and helped me embrace preaching as my profession.

I have found that God will place the right people in your path precisely at the time you need them. Ten years ago I attended a conference in South Africa that was sponsored by the Reverend Jessica Ingram. When she found out I had registered for the event, she invited me to speak. But I was in such a hurtful place in my life, I couldn't do it. It's hard to encourage people when you're all broken up and hurting inside. I felt very much like Naomi when she said that God had dealt with her harshly. Despite my best efforts, I felt like a failure. When I told Rev. Jessica what was going on in my life, the roles reversed. She became the one encouraging me. I told her about a decision I made that resulted in huge financial and personal losses. The fallout was noticeable. Friends walked away from me. I felt hurt and alone. But Rev. Jessica showed up in my life at the precise moment I needed her.

She told me how to get back to a place of wholeness. She assured me that God wasn't going to revoke my calling to preach the gospel. She talked; I listened and heeded her advice. Our mentoring relationship was successful because I had a teachable spirit in a very hurtful time.

My mentors are honest and sometimes vulnerable with me. I remember when the Reverend Elaine Flake, who co-pastors The Greater Allen A.M.E. Church with her husband, former US Congressman Floyd Flake, shared with me some of her experiences co-pastoring with her husband so I'd know how to work with my husband in ministry and not "kill him"! I embraced her discourse on leading from the second chair, and it helped me clarify my role and responsibilities. I can laugh about it now, but thank God for her advice.

Naomi Mentors Ruth

Mentoring requires that a person be open to the instruction of another person and that the mentor have the mentee's best interest at heart. Your mentor is not in competition with you, and a godly mentor would never be jealous of your success. She will listen, learn, and then prayerfully share what she believes God is saying concerning your life. For you, maybe that's how to be a better mother or how to deal with a difficult coworker. In the case of Ruth, God was leading Naomi to give Ruth instructions that would later result in Ruth's getting married.

The Lord's plan began to unfold when Ruth told Naomi she was going to the fields to pick up leftover grain, which was intentionally left for needy widows, orphans, and strangers to glean:

> Naomi said to her, "Go ahead, my daughter." So she went out, entered a field and began to glean behind the harvesters. As it turned out, she was working in a field belonging to Boaz, who was from the clan of Elimelek.
>
> Just then Boaz arrived from Bethlehem and greeted the harvesters, "The LORD be with you!" "The LORD bless you!" they answered.
>
> Boaz asked the overseer of his harvesters, "Who does that young woman belong to?" The overseer replied, "She is the Moabite who came back from Moab with Naomi. She said, 'Please let me glean and gather among the sheaves behind the harvesters.' She came into the field and has remained

110

here from morning till now, except for a short rest
in the shelter."
—Ruth 2:2–7, niv

I love it when a plan comes together! Boaz immediately noticed Ruth working in the field. He immediately
showed her kindness by telling her to glean only in his
field and to follow behind the women who worked for
him. He told the men not to lay a hand on Ruth, and
he gave her permission to get water whenever she was
thirsty.

Boaz assured Ruth that if she worked in his field, she
would have a steady job, protection from the men, and
water to drink. He also thanked her for what she had
done for Naomi, how she left her family back in Moab
to move to Bethlehem to take care of her mother-in-law.
Many sermons suggest that because Boaz and Ruth's
story is a romance, Ruth must have been beautiful, but
the Bible never speaks of her beauty, only her character.

The grace Ruth received from Boaz reminds me of the
grace and kindness Ruth had shown to her mother-in-
law. Ruth planted seeds of kindness in her mother-in-
law's life, and she was beginning to reap a blessing in
her own. It did not matter that Ruth was from a hea-
then country known for its worship of pagan gods. Her
character spoke for itself. This is what will happen to us
when we go where God tells us to go and remain committed to what He has called us to. God will meet our
every need.

Naomi knew Ruth had a teachable spirit. It's a quality
that is lacking in many people today. They want to do
things their way and don't want to listen to the voice

of maturity and wisdom. I've been on both sides of the mentoring relationship, and I can tell you that some people won't follow another person's guidance because they think the individual is too strict, harsh, or limiting in some situations. But listening to and following a mentor's instructions can help a person fulfill her purpose. God works through people.

The Lord put it in Naomi's heart to teach Ruth how to get Boaz's attention. Ruth said to Naomi, "I will do whatever you say" (Ruth 3:5). And she did. Ruth bathed, sprinkled on perfume, put on her best attire, and then went to the threshing floor, where she kept her identity from Boaz a secret until everyone was asleep, just as Naomi had instructed. After Boaz ate, drank, and was in good spirits, he went to sleep near a pile of grain. Naomi had told Ruth that when Boaz was asleep, she was to uncover his feet and lie down there.

When Boaz awoke and saw a stranger sleeping near his feet, he was startled and asked Ruth her name. She answered him, and then she did the unthinkable: she asked Boaz to "cover" her, since he was a kinsman-redeemer!

A kinsman-redeemer is a near male relative who has the "responsibility to act for a relative who was in trouble, danger, or need of vindication."[6] The Hebrew word translated "redeem" in Ruth 3 is *ga'al*, which also can mean "ransom."[7] The near kinsman also had the option to relinquish his claim as a kinsman-redeemer. Boaz explained this to Ruth:

And he said, Who art thou? And she answered, I am Ruth thine handmaid: spread therefore thy skirt over thine handmaid; for thou art a near kinsman. And he said, Blessed be thou of the LORD, my daughter: for thou hast shewed more kindness in the latter end than at the beginning, inasmuch as thou followedst not young men, whether poor or rich. And now, my daughter, fear not; I will do to thee all that thou requirest: for all the city of my people doth know that thou art a virtuous woman. And now it is true that I am thy near kinsman: howbeit there is a kinsman nearer than I. Tarry this night, and it shall be in the morning, that if he will perform unto thee the part of a kinsman, well; let him do the kinsman's part: but if he will not do the part of a kinsman to thee, then will I do the part of a kinsman to thee, as the LORD liveth: lie down until the morning.

—RUTH 3:9–13, KJV

This was a risky move, for sure. Boaz could have misunderstood Ruth's intentions and yelled at her, waking up the other workers asleep on the threshing floor. He could have assumed she was a harlot, but he did no such thing. He had been watching her and knew she was no prostitute. Instead, he called her "a woman of noble character."

This beautiful love story was put in the Bible for a number of reasons, but one of the most important is that it shows us a picture of Jesus. He is our kinsman-redeemer. He shed His precious blood as a ransom for our sins and has redeemed us as His bride.

BOAZ REDEEMS RUTH

When Ruth returned from the threshing floor, she told her mother-in-law what Boaz had said to her and that he had given her six measures of barley to give to Naomi to show that he also cared about her well-being. After hearing this, Naomi told Ruth to do what I believe all Christian mentors should tell the women they mentor: "wait." We must learn to wait on the Lord to hear accurately what He is saying and what He wants us to do. Trust me, you'll experience less heartbreak and more peace in your life if you do. This is why I'm thankful for the Reverend Connie Jackson.

I've known the Reverend Connie Jackson since I was fourteen years old. She's what I call my clarifier. Whenever I feel God is speaking to me about something major about to happen in my life, I turn to Rev. CJ. She doesn't give me the conclusion; she has helped me think through the plethora of things God has said to me. I pray about it, wait, gauge what I believe God is saying by the Word, and then make my own decisions. I believe every woman needs a Rev. CJ in her life.

In Ruth's case, she was instructed to wait for Boaz to ask his relative if he was going to perform his kinsman duty and purchase Elimelek's property and all that belonged to his late sons. I know that waiting on the Lord can be challenging at times, but it's important because your very future depends on it. The next day Boaz went to the city gate and did all that he had promised Ruth, and the nearest kinsman relinquished his right to all that belonged to the family of Elimelek (Ruth 4:2–9).

In Ruth 4:10 Boaz announced to everyone at the city gate that Ruth was to be his wife! The Bible goes on to say that after Boaz and Ruth got married, they had a son named Obed, who became the father of Jesse, who became the father of David, who became one of Israel's greatest kings. Generations later Jesus the Messiah would be born in the lineage of King David. Not only did God bless Ruth with a child; He restored Naomi to a place of joy and peace in her old age for all the women to see. Ruth 4:14–15 says, "The women said to Naomi: 'Praise be to the LORD, who this day has not left you without a guardian-redeemer. May he become famous throughout Israel! He will renew your life and sustain you in your old age. For your daughter-in-law, who loves you and who is better to you than seven sons, has given him birth'" (NIV).

Ruth reaped unthinkable blessing because she allowed herself to be used in the most remarkable way, to transform Naomi's bitter life back to a place of fullness and pleasantness. She was totally committed and followed Naomi back to Bethlehem, knowing she might never see her own family again. Most people would have chosen the easy way out and remained in Moab, but Ruth chose the hard path, the path of sacrifice. And because she did what seemed unthinkable, she ended up in the lineage of Jesus.

———————

Do the Unthinkable

Commit Your Ways to the Lord

Commit everything you do to the LORD. Trust
him, and he will help you.
—PSALM 37:5

Commitment isn't popular. People change jobs, spouses,
likes, interests, and attentions whenever the situation
stops "working" for them. Commitment isn't popular
because it isn't easy, which is why David's words in
Psalm 37:5 are so important for us to remember.

When God leads us to do something unthinkable, it's
easy to try to figure out how to make it happen with our
own strength and resources. But the psalmist encourages us to commit everything we do to the Lord and to
trust Him, and He will help us.

The Hebrew word translated "commit" in this verse is
galal, and it literally means "to roll or to roll away." The
idea is that we are to roll everything about our lives from
ourselves onto God, as if transferring a heavy burden.[8]
When we trust Him with everything we do—every
aspect of our lives—"he will help [us]." Other translations are more specific about what this help looks like.
The New King James Version says, "He shall bring it to
pass," and the New International Version says, "He will
do this."

When we commit ourselves to the Lord, He will bring
to pass His plans for our lives. God wants to see us

operate in our purpose, and our commitment to Him opens the door for Him to align everything in our lives just as He wants it.

There's something else we must keep in mind about commitment. Just as we can trust God to keep His word, people should be able to count on us to follow through with our commitments. My grandfather used to tell all his grandchildren that having a good name is always connected to being a person who honors his or her word. People need to know they can depend on you.

As I mentioned, commitment is hard, but we don't have to do it on our own. I have discovered that when I ask God to help me keep my word, I am able to be consistent. Naomi could depend upon Ruth. It wasn't a temporary thing; Ruth was in it for the long haul. That's what commitment really is.

Commit your ways to the Lord, and ask Him to help you keep your commitments to others. He wants you to trust Him with every area of your life so He can bring His will for you to pass.

CHAPTER 7

UNTHINKABLE WORSHIP
THE WOMAN WITH THE ALABASTER JAR

When a certain immoral woman from that city heard
he was eating there, she brought a beautiful alabaster
jar filled with expensive perfume. Then she knelt
behind him at his feet, weeping. Her tears fell on his
feet, and she wiped them off with her hair. Then she kept
kissing his feet and putting perfume on them....And
Jesus said to the woman, "Your faith has saved you."

—LUKE 7:37–38, 50

W HO DOES SHE think she is, walking in here like
we don't know what she did to get that expensive
jar of perfume? Look at her. She has some nerve getting
that close to Rabbi. Has she no shame? Why is Rabbi
letting her touch Him anyway? He should know better,

being that He is a prophet of God. I've never seen such mockery in all of Israel. This is unthinkable!"

The Bible has no record that those words were ever spoken, but I imagine more than one person had those very thoughts when a certain woman entered the home of Simon the Pharisee. The King James Version of the Bible refers to the woman as a "sinner," but other translations call her an "immoral woman," which is why many theologians think she was a prostitute. We don't know for certain what sins she was guilty of committing, but whatever she did, she was notorious for her deeds. And her notoriety would only increase.

> One of the Pharisees asked Jesus to have dinner with him, so Jesus went to his home and sat down to eat. When a certain immoral woman from that city heard he was eating there, she brought a beautiful alabaster jar filled with expensive perfume. Then she knelt behind him at his feet, weeping. Her tears fell on his feet, and she wiped them off with her hair. Then she kept kissing his feet and putting perfume on them.
>
> When the Pharisee who had invited him saw this, he said to himself, "If this man were a prophet, he would know what kind of woman is touching him. She's a sinner!"
>
> — LUKE 7:36–39

WHAT'S IN A NAME?

Before we delve into this woman's story, I want to draw your attention to something obvious that can actually be easy to overlook. This woman is called many things—"sinner," "immoral woman"—but we never actually learn her name. The fact that she remains nameless in the Bible is in no way a reflection of the significance of this woman's story. I actually believe her name was withheld by design, especially if you consider the importance of a name.

One of a new mother's first acts is to name her child. Right after He created man, God named him Adam. In Genesis 2:19 God created all the animals and birds of the earth and then brought them to Adam so he could give them a name. A name reveals a person's identity and often even their personality and character.

I find it interesting when I meet people who act according to the meaning of their names. For instance, I have a friend I've known since high school whose name is Faith. The word *faith* means "belief and trust in and loyalty to God,"[1] and that describes Faith to a tee. Not only does she trust Jesus as her Savior, but her other friends also trust her with their most private secrets because she is a trustworthy person.

There's also the Old Testament figure Jacob, whose name means "deceiver."[2] Jacob proved true to his name when he deceived his father, Isaac, into giving him his brother's birthright blessing in Genesis 27:36. A name can shape our identity, which is why Jabez, whose name means "pain,"[3] famously asked God to bless him and enlarge his territory "and keep [him] from all trouble and pain!" (1 Chron. 4:10). He no longer wanted "pain" to define him.

We can't choose the names our parents give us, but we can decide how we will be known. Proverbs 22:1 says, "Choose a good reputation over great riches; being held in high esteem is better than silver or gold."

The woman who wept at Jesus's feet in Luke 7 "was [known as] a sinner" (v. 37, AMP), and she wanted a new reputation, which is why I believe the Bible's exclusion of her name was actually an act of God's mercy and grace.

In John 4:16–18 Jesus questioned the woman at the well about her five husbands, thus exposing her immoralities but not her name. Four chapters later, in John 8:3–11, the Pharisees—in an attempt to trap Jesus into contradicting the Law of Moses—questioned Him about a woman who had been caught "in the act" of adultery. Again, Christ addressed the woman's sin and the hypocrisy of the Pharisees who could hardly wait to stone her to death, but He did not say her name. I believe Jesus did not say the names of any of these women because when He shed light on their sinful nature and they accepted the gift of forgiveness He offered, their identities changed forever.

They no longer were defined by their past; they had been transformed by God's power. The Greek term for "transformed" is *metamorphoō*.[4] It's where we get the word *metamorphosis*, which means "change of physical form, structure, or substance especially by supernatural means."[5]

Do you remember the day you accepted Christ into your life? I do, and I can tell you that when I said yes to Him, I changed! I was still Mia on the outside, but the Holy Spirit had invaded my life and given me a new nature. My trust and confidence was in God and not in man. I left a doomed relationship and made decisions for my life that were timely and smart. My choices changed. As a result of my own transformation, I now inspire women to discover their purpose and relationship with God through an organization I founded and lead called Metamorphosis Conference Inc.

Second Corinthians 5:17 says, "Anyone who belongs to Christ has become a new person. The old life is gone; a new life has begun!" This reminds me of the woman at the well. After her conversation with Jesus, her identity changed from that of an adulterer to a missionary who boldly testified to other Samaritans about the power of God. And the same transformation happened to the woman who had been caught in the act of adultery in John 8. Jesus showed her His compassion instead of condemnation, and as a result we don't read anywhere in Scripture that she went back to being a home-wrecker. She too received a new identity because of the grace and mercy of God.

Remember in the chapter about Ruth that I talked about my struggle to rebrand myself and understand who I was and who I was to become in a new season of life? I had gone from being a corporate executive making a great income to trying to figure out a new role and a new call. But God showed me that even though my job title had changed, my spiritual identity was still the same, and without my 9-to-5 I could be even more effective in ministry.

Maybe you secretly struggle with your identity the way I once did. Honestly I believe all women struggle with who they are at one time or another. Our roles in life will change, but whose we are will never change. The nameless woman's struggle ended when she let go of her past and boldly walked into Simon's house to claim her new identity. To become women who do the unthinkable, we must let the Holy Spirit do a deep work in us. At the feet of Jesus, as she poured her love on Jesus, this woman was changed. The love of Jesus broke her and made her new, and it will do the same for you.

SHE GAVE HER ALL IN WORSHIP TO JESUS

It was customary for common people to attend the dinners of affluent residents like Simon, but they were supposed to sit quietly and observe. They weren't welcome at the dinner table, much less allowed to touch the guest of honor.[6] That this woman dared to show up—at the table—was unthinkable.

Some commentaries suggest she went to the dinner because she knew Christ from a previous encounter or conversation, but Scripture does not make that clear. If they had met and He already knew her, surely He would have healed her broken heart and lavished upon her His unconditional love. I believe it's impossible for us to be in the presence of the Lord and not be radically transformed by Him. Even if a person chooses to reject Christ, he or she will never be the same when the Lord makes His presence known. Could it be that word had spread quickly about the miracles Christ performed and this woman wanted Him to do for her what He had done for others?

When the centurion sent word to Jesus that his beloved servant was sick to the point of death, Christ simply spoke the word, and the servant was healed (Luke 7:10). When Jesus was on His way to the town of Nain, He stopped a funeral procession to raise a widow's son from the dead (Luke 7:13–16). And let's not forget about Lazarus. Christ raised him from the dead after he had been in the grave for four long days (John 11:40–44). This unnamed woman had no doubt heard about all the miracles, and she wanted Jesus to touch her life too.

I don't know if the woman ran through the city or walked, but when she entered Simon's house, she found Jesus reclining at the table. The woman was so humbled at the sight of the Savior that she refused to stand in His presence; instead, she knelt at His feet, just weeping. Our tears are never wasted, as Psalm 56:8 says: "You keep track of all my sorrows. You have collected all my tears in your bottle. You have recorded each one in your book."

Christ knew every tear she offered in sacrifice to Him. And when her precious tears fell upon His feet, she dried them with her hair. In biblical times it was a disgrace for a woman to wear her hair down in public, but this woman had no shame. She left it at the feet of Christ, along with all the hurt, loneliness, rejection, embarrassment, and fear that had diminished her self-worth. The Bible says a woman's hair is her glory, and this woman was using her glory to worship the King of kings and Lord of lords, whether or not she knew at the time that she was bowing to royalty.

Luke 7:38 says, "Then she kept kissing His feet and putting perfume on them." She didn't kiss His feet one time; she did it over and over again. How often do we slip to our knees to thank the Lord for being so kind and merciful to us? How often do we thank Him for taking our place on the cross? He was perfect in all His ways, yet He was tortured by Roman soldiers like a criminal so we wouldn't have to pay the price for our sins.

When is the last time we showed our gratitude for the peace and joy we experience every day as a result of the liberty we have in Christ? People worship God in many different ways: through song, prayer, personal sacrifice, financial giving, and more. But our worship should always be a reflection of a grateful heart. Many Christians believe worship is something we do when we go to church on Sunday mornings. It is, but it's so much more than that. Worship is a way of life for the believer.

How Much Is Your Worship Worth?

During my travels to Africa I was given a globe of the world that was made from alabaster, which is a type of mineral that has gypsum or lime sulfate in it.[7] If you're familiar with plaster, think of what that looks like. Alabaster is used to make substances such as plaster. It was also used in Old and New Testament times to construct certain types of buildings in places such as ancient Egypt. It was white and pliable, which would explain why people in biblical days used it to make things such as the jar the woman in our story was carrying.

Inside her jar was perfume that cost a lot of money. Some commentaries say it could have cost as much as a year's wages. I don't know how she got the money to pay for the perfume. Whether she was a prostitute or worked a regular 9-to-5 job to earn the money, it doesn't matter how she got the perfume. What matters is that she sacrificed to the Lord something of great value. What an expression of love! She worshipped Jesus with all she had—her tears, her kisses, and her perfume. When we give God all of ourselves, we open ourselves to receive all that He has to offer. And as this woman worshipped Jesus with a pure heart and so much love, He forgave her sins.

But not everyone recognized what Jesus saw in the woman. The Bible says, "When the Pharisee who had invited him saw this, he said to himself, 'If this man were a prophet, he would know what kind of woman is touching him. She's a sinner!'" (Luke 7:39). Of course Jesus knew the man's thoughts, and He was quick to set the record straight.

> Then Jesus answered his thoughts. "Simon," he said to the Pharisee, "I have something to say to you."
>
> "Go ahead, Teacher," Simon replied.
>
> Then Jesus told him this story: "A man loaned money to two people—500 pieces of silver to one and 50 pieces to the other. But neither of them could repay him, so he kindly forgave them both, canceling their debts. Who do you suppose loved him more after that?"
>
> Simon answered, "I suppose the one for whom he canceled the larger debt."
>
> "That's right," Jesus said. Then he turned to the woman and said to Simon, "Look at this woman kneeling here. When I entered your home, you didn't offer me water to wash the dust from my

feet, but she has washed them with her tears and
wiped them with her hair. You didn't greet me
with a kiss, but from the time I first came in, she
has not stopped kissing my feet. You neglected the
courtesy of olive oil to anoint my head, but she
has anointed my feet with rare perfume.

"I tell you, her sins—and they are many—have
been forgiven, so she has shown me much love.
But a person who is forgiven little shows only little
love." Then Jesus said to the woman, "Your sins
are forgiven."

The men at the table said among themselves,
"Who is this man, that he goes around forgiving
sins?" And Jesus said to the woman, "Your faith
has saved you; go in peace."

—LUKE 7:40–50

I love that Jesus spoke directly to the woman. He
spoke to her for all of us who are eager to know what it
takes to obtain a new identity in Christ. When Simon
got indignant about the woman's worship, Jesus dis-
cerned his thoughts and defended her. He defended her
actions, her sacrifice of expensive perfume, her dem-
onstrative worship, and her love for Him. She had been
forgiven of so much that she loved Him that much more.

This is what a relationship with Christ should look
like. Unlike Simon, she wasn't thinking about all the
religious rules in the Law of Moses: "Don't go here,"
"Don't eat that," "Don't worship on the Sabbath," and on
and on. In fact, this woman wasn't even Jewish; she was
a Gentile. Yet she had been around enough Pharisees to
know she didn't want what they had to offer. Their rules
had never made her feel loved the way Jesus did. She

was the person in the parable with the huge debt of five hundred pieces of silver that couldn't be repaid. But she knew Jesus had paid her debt in full, and all she wanted to do was worship Him.

BEWARE OF SNAKES IN THE CHURCH

As a result of the woman's worship, Jesus rewarded her with a new identity. But His response to Simon should be a warning to all who seek after empty religion instead of a right relationship with the Lord. The first thing Christ did was give Simon a crash course in hospitality, but more importantly He exposed the sin in his heart. In the parable Simon obviously represented the person with the smaller debt of fifty pieces of silver. The unnamed woman was so grateful to have had her debts canceled that she bowed at the creditor's feet in gratitude, worshipping Him and kissing His feet repeatedly.

Simon, on the other hand, did not love Jesus, and the Lord knew it. When you invite someone to your house for dinner, the first thing you do is open the door and welcome the person into your home. You offer to take his coat and ask if there's anything you can do to make him comfortable. Simon did no such thing. He didn't give Jesus water to wash His feet. Nor did he greet Him with a kiss, as was customary. I believe Simon's response to Jesus at the dinner was a reflection of His blackened heart. He refused to repent of his sins and ask the Lord to save him.

Revelation 3:20–21 says Jesus is knocking on the door of every person's heart: "Look! I stand at the door and knock. If you hear my voice and open the door, I will come in, and we will share a meal together as friends. Those who are victorious will sit with me on my throne, just as I was victorious and sat with my Father on his throne." In the parable Simon had a debt of fifty pieces of silver. Even though his debt was smaller than the woman's, he still had a debt he couldn't repay! Not only did he question Jesus's authority as a prophet, but he also proved he had a judgmental spirit. It's the same spirit that continues to permeate the church today.

I remember one year when a friend invited his new girlfriend to the church. She started attending regularly, but it was obvious that she had no experience in church. The clothes she wore were very inappropriate for church. Several of the women came to me asking me if I would talk to her. Of course I too had noticed the clothes and thought very seriously about talking to her, but when I prayed about it, I felt as if the Holy Spirit was leading me to only pray for her and not approach her.

Then one day I cleaned out my closet, and the following Sunday I asked her if she would like me to pass along some clothes to her. She cried. As her eyes filled up with tears, she said, "I know that the women here are looking at me, but I don't have anything else to wear. Thank you for not condemning me but offering me something appropriate."

Soon she became an active member of the church, and her whole family joined because of her. I think about it often, and I wonder if I had approached her differently where she would be. Would I have bruised her developing faith and kept her from experiencing a loving Christian community? Don't get in the way of the Holy Spirit. Let Him do His work in our lives. Be sensitive to God, and know that you are not called to be a Pharisee. I believe we Christians have the perfect solution for a lost and dying world. It's called the "good news" because Jesus willingly died on the cross for our sins, was buried, and was resurrected by the power of God. This is, in fact, good news for humanity because it means we can access God's free gift of salvation. But not every believer does a good job of communicating the message. Scripture says that "all wicked actions are sin" (1 John 5:17), but we tend to treat people as if they cannot be redeemed. What about so-called Christians who are guilty of the same thing?

According to a study by the research firm Barna Group, 64 percent of one thousand Christian men who had been surveyed admitted to watching pornography on a monthly basis. The study also found that the men watched porn at work at the same rate as men who didn't believe in Christ.[8] I could cite one study after another, but what does this one tell us? That modern-day Simons in the church have no right to look down their self-righteous, judgmental noses at people who need to be delivered from the same strongholds they battle.

I close my examination of Simon with this question: Why did he really invite Christ to his home for dinner? Did he want to use Jesus for show-and-tell so he could brag to his neighbors that the Rabbi who could raise the dead was having dinner at his house? Maybe Simon wanted to know what it was like to have a conversation with the Son of God. No, that wasn't it. He wasn't even convinced that Jesus was a prophet, much less the preincarnate God. Did

Simon invite Jesus so he could trick Him into a theological debate and use His answers against Him later? The Bible doesn't tell us why Christ was invited, but judging from the conversation between Simon and Jesus, Simon was no different from other Pharisees.

Jesus often rebuked the Pharisees for their hypocrisy and for abusing the Old Testament Law by using it to condemn others of sinning when they, themselves, were just as guilty. In Matthew 23:33 Christ all but told the Pharisees that they were going to hell when He said: "Snakes! Sons of vipers! How will you escape the judgment of hell?" If you ever get close enough to a snake to see its mouth, you'll notice that it has a "forked" tongue, meaning the tip is split in two like the tines of a fork. This tongue is actually quite amazing because snakes can detect smells with it. When a snake strikes its tongue at the air, its forked tongue allows it to capture two different smells at one time.[9] When Jesus called the Pharisees vipers, He was really calling them venomous hypocrites who preached one thing but did another.

It's Time to Sit at His Feet

Like many of the other stories shared in this book, this woman's story circles around to her faith. When discussing this account, most people focus on the precious ointment she poured on Jesus's feet, but that perfume was not the only thing she sacrificed. She also ended up sacrificing herself. She could have talked herself out of going to the dinner to avoid embarrassment. Instead, she boldly worshipped at Jesus's feet in front of many who condemned her for doing so.

Ten-time Grammy Award–winner CeCe Winans beautifully captured the essence of this nameless woman's story in a song she recorded called "Alabaster Box." I remember the first time I really listened to the lyrics. I was driving on the highway, and when I began to really hear what the song was saying, tears started to stream down my face. I pulled off into the parking lot of a bookstore and replayed the song over and over. Thoughts about my past—the shameful moments and poor decisions I had made in life—were racing through my mind. I didn't want anybody to know about those secret things. But the song reminded me that God knew it all yet still loved me! I could not help but feel both broken and joyful as the song retold this woman's story.

Incredibly thousands of years later worshipping at the feet of Jesus is still the only way to find everlasting peace and forgiveness from our sins. God wants to invade your life and have an authentic, intimate relationship with you. I say authentic because technically, you may have already invited Christ into your heart as your Savior—but that's not the end; it's the beginning. There's more—much more!

God created us to be in relationship with Him. Don't think that He needs us, because He doesn't. He wants us just as He wanted a relationship with the unnamed woman in this chapter. Greater intimacy, spiritual break-throughs, and so much more await you. But you'll have to push past the snakes in your life to get what the Lord has for you. The nameless woman with the alabaster jar had forgiveness, salvation, intimacy, and intimate worship at Jesus's feet waiting for her. What awaits you? Run to Him, and you'll discover how much He loves you. Don't let the Simons in your church, on your job, or in your mind hold you back.

Get on your knees ASAP, and give Him your best sacrifice. Give Him you.

DO THE UNTHINKABLE

Give God Your Heart

> The sacrifice you desire is a broken spirit. You will not reject a broken and repentant heart, O God.
> —PSALM 51:17

It wasn't until I was deeply offended and the person who wronged me bought me a gift that I really understood the implication of this scripture. I recognized that this person wasn't trying to repair the broken relationship; this individual was just trying to make things seem OK by offering a token. That gift did nothing to improve the situation because it was given without sincerity.

In the same manner God isn't looking for religious tokens from us; He doesn't need gifts and sacrifices given without conviction. The sacrifice God wants is our hearts. He wants us to bring our hearts to Him, broken and humble, so He can refill them with His love. Just like clay on the potter's wheel, He can reshape your life and make it new—if you let Him. It's unthinkable.

CHAPTER 8

UNTHINKABLE FORGIVENESS
JOSEPH

But Joseph replied, "Don't be afraid of me. Am I God, that I can punish you? You intended to harm me, but God intended it all for good. He brought me to this position so I could save the lives of many people."

—Genesis 50:19–20

SEATED AT THE dinner table were the very ones who had harmed him. These men were his brothers, but they had caused him more pain than he once may have thought possible. They had left him for dead before selling him into slavery in Egypt, where he was falsely accused, tossed into prison, and forgotten about for what must have seemed like an eternity. But that wasn't even the worst of it. His brothers had robbed him of more than a decade with their father. Jacob hadn't been able to see his son grow into a man, marry the woman of his choosing, and build his own family. They stole the life Joseph might have had. Indeed, everyone back home thought he was dead. In effect, he was dead.

Seeing his brothers again was hard, but when they returned with his youngest brother, Benjamin, it was too much. Joseph had dinner served to his brothers, but he rushed to his chambers, needing time to himself, time to let out the tears that he could no longer hold back. Alone in his room, Joseph wept bitterly. They say time has a way of healing old wounds, but this wound oozed freely, painfully, as if everything had just happened.

The first time Joseph saw his brothers in Egypt was nearly two decades after they sold him into slavery. All of them were grown men by that time; some were even grandfathers. Despite the years, the aging, and the distance, Joseph recognized them as his brothers. Yet they saw only a powerful Egyptian who had food they could buy amid a terrible famine.

Joseph had a new name, Zaphenath-Paneah, which means "God speaks."[1] He had an Egyptian wife and family. By no means did he appear to be anyone other than the second–most powerful man in Egypt. These Hebrew travelers had no idea the man to whom they had bowed was actually their brother.

Upon seeing his brothers, Joseph needed a way to keep them close, so he devised a plan. He inquired about his younger brother, Benjamin, and his father and required his brothers to bring Benjamin to Egypt if they were to receive any more aid. He was glad to hear his brother and father were alive and well, but he had to see Benjamin for himself.

His scheme to keep Simeon in Egypt until the other brothers returned with Benjamin actually worked, and they didn't suspect a thing. And now they were all back in his dining room, even Benjamin. It was overwhelming. Behind the mask of success and power was still a seventeen-year-old who had lost everything because he shared his dreams with spiteful siblings.

All the bad things that had happened to him in the last nineteen years must have been at the forefront of his mind as he stood in his room weeping. I imagine his blood was pumping through his veins like a racehorse on its final turn. Seeing Benjamin was a stark reminder of all he had lost, all the moments he had missed out on.

Yet as much as Joseph might have wanted to hate his brothers for all the hurt they caused him, he couldn't. Not really. He knew that if it had not been for their evil plan, he wouldn't have been in his current position. God had given him dreams of this very point in his life, when his brothers would bow to him. His family thought his dreams were crazy; his brothers even tried to kill him because of them. Yet he still could not hate them.

Later, after Joseph tricked his brothers into thinking he was going to take Benjamin prisoner, he decided to give up the charade. He probably wasn't sure what he would say or if his brothers would even believe him. But he knew who he was, so he simply said, "I am Joseph, your brother, whom you sold into slavery in Egypt. But don't be upset, and don't be angry with yourselves for selling me to this place. It was God who sent me here ahead of you to preserve your lives" (Gen. 45:4–5).

As Joseph spoke words of forgiving kindness to the same men who could not speak a kind word to him, he embraced each of his brothers, kissing and weeping over them. I can imagine how Joseph must have felt in that moment—liberated, free. I know because I've experienced the power of forgiveness, and I know how life-changing it can be.

What Was He Thinking?

To be honest, I wrestled with whether to include Joseph in this book. When I began to list all the biblical figures whose unthinkable acts brought extraordinary results, everyone on my list was female. That was by design. I loved the idea of exploring the lives of amazing women whose example can teach us still today. But I couldn't shake the story of Joseph.

Although I dramatized Joseph's story some at the beginning of this chapter, it is no exaggeration that Joseph's brothers caused him tremendous pain. It's hard to avoid pain in life. We all face it in one way or another. People hurt us, and sometimes the pain can be so unbearable we think we'll never find our way out. What's even worse is when we have no idea why we're being treated so badly. We mentally sort through all our misdeeds to find some explanation. "What did I do to deserve this?" we wonder. I've asked that question many times. You may have wondered the same thing yourself.

I imagine Joseph asked himself that question too. He faced one hardship after another through no fault of his own, and his problems started long before he was born. Joseph's family had some serious dysfunction. His father, Jacob, had married two sisters, Rachel and Leah, and they spent much of their adult lives vying for his love and attention.

This wasn't the life Jacob intended. Jacob loved Rachel deeply, so much that he agreed to work for her father, Laban, for seven years in order to make her his wife. But when the seven years came to an end, Laban tricked Jacob and deceitfully married him off to Rachel's older sister, Leah. Jacob had no desire to be married to Leah; he wanted to marry Rachel. So he agreed to work another seven years to make her his wife.

This was just the beginning of Jacob's problems. Now with two wives, Jacob found himself in a real-life tug-of-war. The Bible says God closed Rachel's womb, which means she was unable to give Jacob the sons she knew he desperately wanted. Meanwhile, Leah also found herself in a difficult position. She was unloved, and she knew it, and because of that the Bible says God opened her womb. Leah's ability to have children was remarkable. She made childbearing look easy, having son after son while Rachel remained barren and broken in spirit.

Desperate to give her husband a child, Rachel came up with a "brilliant" idea that wasn't so brilliant at all. She decided to give her servant Bilhah to Jacob and allow him to have children with her. Not to be outdone by her sister, Leah decided to do the same thing. The result was more children and more strife.

Then after Leah, Bilhah, and Leah's servant Zilpah had given Jacob ten sons, the Bible says:

> God remembered Rachel's plight and answered her prayers by enabling her to have children. She became pregnant and gave birth to a son.
> "God has removed my disgrace," she said. And she named him Joseph, for she said, "May the LORD add yet another son to my family."
> —GENESIS 30:22–24

Imagine Jacob's excitement when he learned of Rachel's news. He already had a houseful of children, but the woman he truly loved was pregnant with his child. His heart beat a little faster; his step got a little lighter. He was delighted, and that is the environment into which Joseph was born.

I'm sure if the mothers were at odds, their children knew of the discord, and they too felt they had to vie for their father's affection. Just as it was clear to everyone that Jacob loved Rachel, it was also clear that he loved Joseph. At one point Jacob even gave Joseph a coat of many colors, and the Bible makes no mention of him giving anything to his other sons. Seeing that Joseph was their father's favorite, Jacob's sons didn't love Joseph as brothers typically would. They saw him as a rival. And that only got worse when God began to give Joseph dreams.

I have to believe that Joseph's dreams were so brilliant and amazing that in his innocence he didn't stop to think how his family might receive them. He probably felt he had to tell the others. The dream with his brothers' bundles of wheat bowing down to his was so vivid, so real, so amazing. And the second, with the sun, moon, and stars bowing to Joseph, was even more incredible. It probably didn't occur to him that others might not think the dreams were so wonderful.

As you might imagine, Joseph's brothers refused to consider even the possibility that the dreams were from God. Instead, they accused Joseph of thinking he was better than they were. Even Jacob scolded Joseph when he heard the dreams, though he did wonder what they meant (Gen. 37:9–11).

Then one day Jacob sent Joseph to check on his brothers, as he commonly did, and bring back a report. As soon as his brothers saw Joseph coming, they called out, "Here comes that dreamer!...Come now, let's kill him and throw him into one of these cisterns and say that a ferocious animal devoured him. Then we'll see what comes of his dreams" (Gen. 37:19–20, NIV).

You may know the rest of the story. Joseph's brothers ultimately pulled him from the cistern and sold him to Midianite traders, who took Joseph into Egypt. Within a short period of time Joseph was put in charge of Potiphar's house. Yet it was there that Potiphar's wife falsely accused Joseph of assaulting her when he refused to give in to her sexual advances.

From Potiphar's house Joseph was thrown into prison. There he interpreted dreams for Pharaoh's cupbearer and baker. Joseph asked that they remember him. But when the two men were released from prison, they promptly forgot about him. Then Pharaoh had a dream no one could understand.

As Egypt's wise men tried in vain to interpret the dream, the cupbearer remembered Joseph and told Pharaoh about him. Joseph was brought from prison to interpret the dream, and because of his ability to discern what God was saying, Joseph was made second-in-command over Egypt.

At every point in Joseph's story we read that God was with him. (See Genesis 39:2, 21; Acts 7:9.) That is how he survived all the hardships he endured and went from the pit to the palace in what seemed like a day. But while it is incredible that Joseph's life took such a dramatic turn for the better, there is something else I want you to see in Joseph's story, something that I think warrants more discussion than it is usually given: Joseph never could have fulfilled his purpose in Egypt if he had not suffered the inexplicable pain his brothers' jealous, hate-filled actions caused him. Their actions pushed him out of his father's house, and had that not happened, he could not have become the man he became.

Many people today also face difficulties in their families—favoritism, inequities, hurt from sensing a lack of love, and more. As the saying goes, we choose our friends, but we cannot choose our families. As a church leader and life coach, I often meet people who have experienced family hurt. That has to be one of the most difficult types of pain to endure. Home is where a person should feel safe, loved, and affirmed, but some people have known only violation there. Anger and jealousy replaced love and affirmation, and hate-filled words cut like knives and left deep, lasting wounds.

But the hurt experienced at home doesn't have to be the end of the story. It doesn't have to become a burden someone always carries. There is a remedy for hurts that don't heal over time, but it's not what most people expect. The way to find wholeness and healing after deep wounding is forgiveness. It is the only way to move forward.

Unforgiveness Is a Poison

Forgive is one of the most powerful words in the English language. It is also one of the most difficult things to do. Sometimes it's unthinkable. You've heard it said that unforgiveness is a poison you drink, thinking the other person will die. When we have been victimized in some way, we feel entitled to hold on to the hurt and pain inflicted. But no one ever succeeds with this plan, and the other person never dies from the poison we drink. Although it seems effective for the moment, the sad reality is that the person who hurt you doesn't die from that poison—you do. Dreams die. Hopes die. Relationships die. Trust dies. In a sense death and unforgiveness go hand-in-hand, but the sad trajectory of hurt and bitterness can be changed by one unthinkable action—forgiveness.

Human nature can be difficult to understand. What is the root of hatred and jealousy? And how do we stomp them out at their core? Jealousy and hatred have been around as long as mankind has existed. In the very first family there was jealousy, envy, and hatred. It was so bad that Cain murdered his brother Abel because God approved of Abel's offering and not his. Perhaps you're not tempted to murder anyone, but slanderous words, hateful actions, and spiteful motives are just as murderous to a person's character and dreams as a loaded gun or a skillfully wielded knife is to someone's life.

Despite all the evil that exists and the terrible things people do to one another, we need to forgive. In fact, we are commanded to do so. Jesus told His disciples, "If you forgive those who sin against you, your heavenly Father will forgive you. But if you refuse to forgive others, your Father will not forgive your sins" (Matt. 6:14–15).

I remember when God began to speak to me about my need to forgive a wrong that had been committed against me. I thought, "Let it go? Really?" But I clearly heard God say, "Yes, let it go." I could hardly believe my ears. "But, Lord!" I lamented. I was so hurt, so broken that I couldn't see the light of day. I just didn't understand why I had to do all the work and let the offense go. The pain of a betrayal, the ongoing maligning of my character seemed too much to handle. I felt as if I were being made out to be the bad guy when, in fact, I was the one who had been wronged. *Why did I have to forgive?*

Months later I discovered the true detriment of unforgiveness when I realized the poison I thought would injure the person who had wounded me had crept into my spirit and emotions. My actions and reactions were shaped by unforgiveness. It seemed my whole world was being reshaped by it. I was cautious of where I went because I worried about whom I might run into and what that person might be thinking. I worried about whether she knew my side of the story or if she believed what the other person had been saying. I was embarrassed and angry at the same time. I felt like it was a shame that I had to go through what I was experiencing. But the day I finally realized how deep the poison had crept into my spirit is the day I prayed God would set me free.

You Choose Your Outcome

I decided to change my outcome. I chose to recognize the hurt and pain that was inflicted upon me but no longer allow it to dictate where I went or how I felt. Yes, it hurt, but in facing the pain, I found freedom. I chose to see the injustice but to not let it have authority over me. When we choose to take authority over our reaction to pain, we choose freedom.

The Mayo Clinic describes *forgiveness* this way:

> Generally, forgiveness is a decision to let go of resentment and thoughts of revenge. The act that hurt or offended you might always remain a part of your life, but forgiveness can lessen its grip on you and help you focus on other, more positive parts of your life. Forgiveness can even lead to feelings of understanding, empathy and compassion for the one who hurt you.
>
> Forgiveness doesn't mean that you deny the other person's responsibility for hurting you, and it doesn't minimize or justify the wrong. You can forgive the person without excusing the act. Forgiveness brings a kind of peace that helps you go on with life.[2]

While I recognized that I had been wronged, I chose to forgive. I let go of any right I felt I had to revenge. Holding on to unforgiveness makes us bitter and angry. I chose to become better, not bitter.

Forgiveness brings freedom.

I've learned that unforgiveness leads to bondage—a bondage I do not want in my life. Forgiveness, on the other hand, leads to freedom. Forgiving broke something for me. The moment I said the words "I forgive," it was almost as if I could hear Jesus on the cross at Calvary asking the Father to forgive us of our sins. (See Luke 23:34.) I felt an instant release. For the first time in months I could exhale.

But even after I chose to forgive, I struggled with what that really meant. Did I need to call my offender? Should I write an email? Was this forgiveness tied to reconciliation? Was I somehow supposed to forget all the hateful and hurtful things that had been done to me? I didn't know where to start walking out the forgiveness I had just proclaimed. So I cried out, "God, please give me some direction."

When I asked God to give me direction, I realized that for me forgiveness meant I would no longer give someone else authority over my life. How I responded, how I thought, how I felt—it was all under a new master. I also learned that forgiveness didn't mean I forgot or condoned what happened; it meant I no longer would be controlled by the pain. In other words, I can't feel the pain I felt then in the same way. When those memories creep in, I say to myself, "God has forgiven me, and I forgive [that person]." I refuse to allow myself to be controlled by that hurt ever again. I allowed God to step in completely, and when I did, He gave me back my peace of mind and truly lifted the weight of that burden off my chest.

Forgiveness lets you off the hook.
One of the greatest benefits of forgiveness is that it releases you from your past pain and suffering. Sometimes we think it is more difficult to forgive because it seems we are letting the other person off the hook for their misdeeds. But to the contrary, it lets *you* off the hook from continued suffering.

As the Mayo Clinic definition noted, forgiving also can help you become more empathetic and compassionate. I always wondered why Joseph's brothers hated him. I thought it was just because his father had given him a coat that was colorful and because his brothers didn't like what his dream suggested—that they would bow down to Joseph. But the animosity started long before the coat or the dream.

Recognizing the tension in the household and the relationship of father to mother makes it a bit easier for me to see why the brothers didn't show Joseph much brotherly love. It isn't always easy to understand why people behave the way they do, but considering their story sometimes helps us better comprehend their actions, although it doesn't mean we will agree with the choices they made. Understanding isn't always easy, but it is possible.

Joseph could have blamed his brothers for sending him down a painful path. He could have lost himself in hatred toward Potiphar's wife, who stole years of his life when her lie landed him in prison. He could have felt less than worthy when he was forgotten in prison. But through it all it seems Joseph chose a better route—the path of forgiveness.

Forgiveness takes strength.

Forgiveness is not for the weak. It takes a strong person to forgive. It really does. Mahatma Gandhi is quoted as saying, "The weak can never forgive. Forgiveness is an attribute of the strong."[3] Recognizing the faults within others can lead to surprising conclusions. It can remind us that we have faults of our own. We likely have inflicted hurts upon others who await our acknowledgment of their pain. It takes strength to admit you have done something wrong.

One of the most powerful and most difficult actions I have taken in my life occurred when I was seeking God for direction about how to be released from the pain others caused me. Instead of telling me how wrong the person who hurt me had been, God pointed His microscope toward me and showed me where I had hurt others. I called the people whom God showed me I had wounded and asked for their forgiveness. As I said, "Please forgive me for my actions or words that offended or harmed you," I could feel God breaking strongholds of hurt and pain in my life.

Let me be honest. When God showed me these people I had wounded, I immediately thought of ways they had offended or hurt me too. The truth be told, relationships are two-way streets. Life is full of actions and reactions. Yet while I may have been hurt, God was showing me that I had retaliated and hurt them in return.

There have been a couple of instances when I knew I had done nothing to justify or even explain the hurtful acts perpetrated against me. Still, God called me to forgive. I didn't call those individuals, but I took the matter to God in prayer and left the situation with Him. Those experiences too were liberating.

When I decided that I no longer would be a victim and would forgive instead, I became victorious. In my spirit I became happier and had more peace. I felt vulnerable, yet empowered, as if I had regained control of my life. I no longer felt as if I was being reactionary. Emotionally and mentally I was free to live my life without the chains of unforgiveness holding me hostage to my past. Freedom is one of the most incredible feelings!

Can you imagine what would have happened if at the dinner table that evening Joseph had chosen to say to his family, "The hatred you had for me I am now going to inflict upon you"? What would have happened to the heritage of Israel? What would have happened to the future of this great people? It might have ended at that dinner table.

But instead of Joseph holding a grudge and desiring to get even with his brothers, he made a profound choice to forgive, and he never wavered. Even years later, after his father had died, Joseph maintained the same commitment. When their father was gone and Joseph's brothers thought he would finally seek vengeance, Joseph told them:

> Don't be afraid of me. Am I God, that I can punish you? You intended to harm me, but God intended it all for good. He brought me to this position so I

could save the lives of many people. No, don't be afraid. I will continue to take care of you and your children.

—GENESIS 50:19–21

The Bible even says he spoke kindly to them. The brothers who could not speak a kind word to Joseph were reassured by Joseph's kind words.

It must have been liberating for Joseph's brothers to know their offense would not be returned upon them. In a way it's like the grace God bestows on each of us. Our sinful offenses toward God should be met with His wrath, but instead they are met with His grace. God clears the offense and takes away the judgment due. I don't know about you, but I am grateful for God's grace and forgiveness. They are beyond amazing.

If we focus on forgiving and the personal power we gain when we release past hurt and pain, our lives will be healthier and more productive. We will indeed be free. Forgiveness was such a part of Joseph's life that he gave his two sons names that would remind him daily of the power he had gained because he chose to forgive. Manasseh, the name given to Joseph's firstborn son, means "causing to forget."[4] And the name of his younger son, Ephraim, means "double fruit."[5] In his sons' names Joseph was saying that God made him forget his pain, gave him the strength to overcome the hardest parts of his life, and blessed him in the land of his bondage. Joseph found the key to overcoming a life filled with hate and hurt when he made the unthinkable choice to forgive.

What about you? Holding on to bitterness and unfor-giveness only releases poison in your life—and the longer you hold on to it, the more poison is released. I believe some of our physical and mental health conditions are caused by the poison unleashed by unforgiveness. It's time to ask God to help you release it. Let it go. Forgive.

Do the Unthinkable

Allow God to Set You Free

And forgive us our sins, as we have forgiven those who sin against us.
—MATTHEW 6:12

She fed me poison, and I drank it. She tried to kill me, but I survived.

At one time I thought I'd never be able to think about what was one of the most difficult times of my life without feeling a tinge of pain. Why would a friend try to poison me with her wicked lies?

But one night as I prayed, asking God to forgive me of my sins, I heard Him say, "Forgive others." When I did what God asked me to do, the unthinkable happened. I was set free. And I didn't just survive—I began to thrive.

What or whom do you need to forgive? Today do the unthinkable, and give the hurt and pain to God. Let it go. Forgive.

CHAPTER 9

AN UNTHINKABLE TOUCH
THE WOMAN WITH THE ISSUE OF BLOOD

*And a woman was there who had been subject to
bleeding for twelve years, but no one could heal her.
She came up behind [Jesus] and touched the edge of
his cloak, and immediately her bleeding stopped.*

—LUKE 8:43–44, NIV

S HE HAD BEEN sick for more than a decade—twelve
years, to be exact. Living day after day with the
same disgusting condition had been devastating to
her physically, emotionally, spiritually, financially, and
socially. The hemorrhaging impacted her life in ways
she had never expected. It had made her anemic, leaving
her feeling weak and drained of energy all the time. She
hardly had enough strength to get out of bed each day.

And if that weren't bad enough, she often lacked the will to get up. Each day she faced the same struggle to get moving, yet somehow she mustered the strength to do it.

As the lingering sickness weakened her body, it had made her increasingly disheartened and depressed. Her unanswered prayers only made her feel worse. She felt ignored, as if she no longer mattered, even to God. She had lost so much over the years, and it seemed as if she would never get better or reclaim what she had lost. Despite her pleas to God, her situation continued— day after day, week after week, month after month, year after year. There was never any change.

If life had not been difficult enough due to her physical issue, she also faced the sociological impact of her illness. Governed by the Law of Moses and restricted by Levitical guidelines on "touching," she was isolated and alone. She was sick—of rules, of doctors, of not having enough money left after paying her medical bills, of not finding a cure, and just of being sick. As my mother used to say, she was sick and tired of being sick and tired.

Have you ever felt that way? No answers for your draining questions. No direction on what to do next. No help. Only a feeling of going deeper and deeper into a place where there seem to be no answers, only more problems. That's what life was for her.

One day when someone told her that Jesus—the man who had performed all kinds of miracles—was coming to town, a glimmer of hope lit in her mind. It began an earnest dialogue in her head, as if two people were sitting across a table from each other, having an intense discussion. One moment she was hopeful; the next, mindful of the rules and laws that governed her situation.

"What if…?" she wondered.

"No, I can't…"

"Why not?" she countered.

"I'm not supposed to!"

"Who's going to know?"

"Everyone will know!"

"Still, what if…?"

Should she conform to the rules that said, "Don't leave your tent; don't spread your uncleanness"? Or should she go find Jesus? Bleeding had impacted the last twelve years of her life. No matter how you look at it—144 months, 624 weeks, or 4,380 days—that's a long time to be dealing with the same issue, and she'd had enough.

An Unthinkable Decision

That day she made an unthinkable decision. Thinking, "If I can only touch His garment, I will be made whole," she decided to do whatever she had to do to touch Jesus. Everything she had been taught was being challenged the moment she made up her mind to get dressed and go see Jesus. But what did she have to lose? She had lost everything, and her situation wasn't getting better.

The Bible never says she was confined to her home, but if she was a good Hebrew woman, then she followed a list of "do nots." She knew she was considered unclean, dirty. And anyone she came in contact with would be made dirty too. The very thought of touching Him—well, it was unthinkable. But she was thinking it!

As she pulled garment after garment out of her wardrobe, she determined to layer herself with enough clothing to disguise who she was and keep people from noticing the bleeding. "This is my last chance," the woman said to herself as she left home. She had no option but to get to the One she believed could heal her disease.

The crowd was bigger than she expected, and He was farther away than she had anticipated. She prayed that no one would recognize her, but her mind was made up: *nothing* was going to stop her. She pressed through the crowd, weaving her way magnificently. Every time a little space opened up, she grabbed it and steadily moved toward Him. She was getting closer! With each step, a rush of adrenaline made her feel stronger, strong enough to ignore the voice in her head telling her to run home before anyone recognized her. "I'll keep going until I touch Him," she told herself again.

As she got close to Him, the wall of people surrounding Him seemed to thicken. When she could not move any farther, she began to crawl along the stone and dirt pathway. Finally she could see Him! She extended her arm through the cloaked legs and sandaled feet of the men surrounding Him and stretched it as far as she could. She didn't know if her hand would reach, but then she felt it with the very tip of her fingers. Not Him, but "it," His robe. She didn't need any more than that. She believed that if she could just touch the hem of His garment, she would be healed.

Immediately she felt different. Healing power ran from her fingertip to her hand, through her arm into her chest, into her abdomen, and to her womb, the source of the cramping and pain. Warmth coursed through her body, and then she felt what she hadn't felt in twelve years. She felt dry.

She remained still, trying to understand what had just happened, but there were voices and people moving around her. The sound seemed to escalate quickly, and she saw Jesus begin to look around. She wasn't sure what was going on. Then she heard Him ask, "Who touched Me?"

Don't Touch—or Else!

Over several hundred years the children of Abraham grew from a people to tribes to the nation of Israel. After generations they finally entered the land promised to their ancestor. But they could not live in the Promised Land without laws. In order for them to function as a nation, rules and laws were established to govern them. In addition to the well-known Ten Commandments given by God to Moses, there were Levitical laws. These were given after the Ten Commandments were established to help the people live in a way that honored God.

None of the commandments and laws were created by men. Rather, they were God-given mandates. The Creator Himself spoke the commandments; He personally delivered them so His people would be governed according to His will and His standard of holiness. In other words, these were no ordinary rules. They were God's laws, given to Moses and Aaron to guard the people from ceremonial uncleanness.

Among the many laws given was one that specifically addressed bodily discharges. In essence, a person experiencing a discharge from his or her body was considered ceremonially unclean. Therefore, anything and anyone that person touched was defiled, making that thing or person also unclean. This concept of being "unclean" went far beyond the idea of "spreading germs." The person and anything he or she touched would be deemed spiritually unclean.

Of the five senses, touch is developed intrauterine and experienced before birth. It is the first connectivity the new life growing in the womb has with his or her mother. Throughout our lives touch develops as a key sense. It is very important because through touch we express our intentions. Touch is a primary part of our humanity. A person can calm the nerves of a loved one by the simple stroke of her hand or by merely touching an arm. And with the same hands a person can express anger by pounding fists on a table. The manner of the touch provokes a certain response. A child touched inappropriately will withdraw. A person touched in love will move closer. Take away the ability to touch another person, and you remove a core aspect of human connectedness.

In essence, this woman was stripped of this important part of being human. She could no longer enjoy the warmth, beauty, and comfort of touch. At a critical time in her life, when a comforting touch was needed more than ever, she was mandated to isolate herself. No hugs from loved ones to let her know everything would be all right. No simple touch on the hand to express care and concern. No kiss on the cheek to say, "It's so good to see you." Nothing. It was the law:

> If a woman has a discharge of blood for many days, other than at the time of her customary impurity, or if it runs beyond her usual time of impurity, all the days of her unclean discharge shall be as the days of her customary impurity. She shall be unclean. Every bed on which she lies all the days of her discharge shall be to her as the bed of her impurity; and whatever she sits on shall be unclean, as the uncleanness of her impurity. Whoever touches those things shall be unclean; he shall wash his clothes and bathe in water, and be unclean until evening.
> —LEVITICUS 15:25–27, NKJV

Most people were taught certain rules as children, the dos and don'ts of life. I know I was. There were certain places in our home that we kids were not allowed to utilize without permission. One in particular was the formal living room. It was used only for special gatherings, such as on Thanksgiving and Christmas, and no one dared to tread upon the neatly lined carpet until the holidays rolled around—or else!

This rule was given because Mom wanted one room where she could showcase her good furniture and china. We were not allowed entry because, as children, we did not appreciate the value of those items, most of which were heirlooms or items that she worked long and hard to purchase. We could not touch anything because she didn't want us to break anything.

One rainy day we kids were playing hide-and-seek inside the house, and I hid in the formal living room. Sure enough, as I'm sure my mother feared, I accidentally bumped into the china cabinet, causing some very fragile plates to topple over. My poor attempt to cover up my misdeed was met with a punishment that I will never forget. Had I stayed in the space where I was allowed to touch things, I would never have gotten into so much trouble that day—and I wouldn't have experienced a different kind of touch from my mom. That touch, also called a spanking, was a constant reminder to respect the house rules and areas deemed off-limits!

Rules create boundaries and establish ways to live. We all are governed by various rules—written and unwritten, spoken and unspoken. Like them or not, agree with the principle of them or not, our lives are bound by rules. And rule breakers are often viewed negatively. That's what this woman feared—scorn for not following the rules.

THE POWER OF TOUCH

Nearly every person I know or have known who has dealt with a long-term illness has experienced the weariness that comes with it. It is natural to long for the illness to be over. No one wants to be sick. The mental toll that comes with physical distress can become a heavy burden in its own right. I have also found that the weariness can affect those around you. Whether you are the patient or the caregiver, you just want the suffering to end.

While I was blessed to care for my mother in her final years, watching Alzheimer's disease steal her life right in front of my eyes was one of the most difficult things I have ever had to endure. She was given the diagnosis at the age of sixty-five, and Mom's body deteriorated rapidly over the next few years. She would lose thoughts and words mid-sentence. She would get frustrated searching for words she once recalled with ease. She'd lose or misplace things, and it would take us weeks to locate them, if we ever did. We never found her cell phone and a few sets of house keys.

The day she got lost was a turning point for all of us. She had driven herself to a midday ministry meeting at church, as she had done for the previous ten years. But this time she didn't arrive. She had become disoriented and was lost for a few hours before she navigated back home. Scared out of our wits, we decided that day that Mom could no longer drive. We just couldn't take the risk of her being lost or harming herself or someone else with a vehicle. That was one of the most difficult paths we had to walk. Telling a once highly self-sufficient woman that she no longer had the privilege of driving was, in effect, taking away her independence. It was the exact opposite of the feeling a newly licensed sixteen-year-old gets upon receiving the right and privilege to drive. She would now have to depend upon others to take her places.

As the Alzheimer's took its toll, Mom became severely depressed, knowing how this illness would ultimately affect her memory and recognition of others. She worked hard to remember names and faces, but eventually her efforts weren't enough to stop the advancement of the disease. She got tired and started praying that God either would heal her or take her to be with Jesus. She just wanted it to be over. But that isn't the nature of this disease. It brings years of deterioration. We all became weary caring for Mom—beyond the point that we were physically able to keep up with the medical need. It was getting harder and harder, but we were determined not to place her in a long-term-care facility.

As caretakers, it was hard for us to go through this and see not just the physical effects but also the mental and emotional damage. No one was ready for Mom to die, but no one wanted her to suffer. It was a labor of love to care for her. We made modifications for her to stay in our home. And with my husband, sister, and brother as well as my children, goddaughter, niece, and her caretakers—literally a whole tribe—we made schedules and adjustments to be with her twenty-four hours a day. I believe she felt the love and care she needed in her final years. But it was hard. We had to make a lot of sacrifices.

There were days when we all didn't get along. We tried to manage our frustrations, but that wasn't always possible. It was hard making life adjustments and cancelling or turning down engagements when there was no one to watch Mom. She needed constant supervision, and everyone in the family worked full time, was in school full time, or lived out of town. Nevertheless, we made it work, and yes, there was a cost. Some of us became sick in the process, succumbing to the pressure and stress. Some suffered financial loss, and some, emotional pain.

Watching my mother's exuberant spirit die inside of a living body was hard. Although for the most part she seemed healthy and strong, as her brain cells began to lose function, her organs and vital systems followed. With her brain's ability to communicate with the rest of her body impaired, one organ system after another shut down.

Mom stopped walking, which meant that we physically had to lift her from the bed to a wheelchair to the tub, table, or toilet, and back again. Daily it was a physical workout. Eventually she stopped talking. The lack of verbal communication was painful. It felt like torture to no longer hear her sweet, melodious voice call out, "Good morning!" or say, "Mia, I love you!" Instead, we all experienced cold silence. There was no more singing from our songbird. Then she stopped eating altogether, and the hospice team began preparing us for her transition. A few weeks later, on September 29, 2012, Mom was surrounded by all her children and grandchildren when she took her final breath and transitioned to heaven.

Her disease affected all five of her senses: seeing, hearing, smelling, tasting, and touching. She kept her eyes closed most of the time, so in time we weren't able to look into her eyes and know that she saw us too. Eventually it seemed that she also stopped listening to what we said. If she did hear us, she stopped responding to what she had heard. We still talked to her and played music for her, but it was hard to tell if she understood anything. Food was no enticement either. She would not smell anything, and her sense of taste had dissipated, so even her favorite foods held no appeal.

But the one sense she never lost was touch. No matter how disengaged Mom seemed, she exhaled at a kiss to the forehead, seemed to smile when we rubbed lotion on her arms and legs, and sighed as we caressed her face and told her we loved her. Just as touch expresses love and safety to a newborn, it communicated the same message to Mom.

A Woman Just Like Us

Twelve years is a long time. Children grow up—toddlers become teens; teenagers become adults. Lives can change significantly in twelve years. Now imagine being sick for twelve years. I mean, really sick. And not getting better. And not just sick physically but also being condemned and confined as a social outcast because of your sickness—for twelve years.

The woman with the issue of blood could have been like any woman with a family and a career. Maybe she loved watching her children grow up and go to school. She was probably a good wife, a good cook; maybe everyone liked to come to her house and have a meal. Even more, maybe this woman worked a job and found a great sense of satisfaction in developing her career. Or perhaps she had a small business of her own, and building her business was a highlight of her life. Perhaps friends and neighbors came to her for assistance because she was gifted with knowledge and always insightful. She may have been pleasant to be around and to work with. Whatever she was like, she was definitely someone we would consider a strong woman—one who took care of her home and managed her own affairs at the same time.

Then one day everything changed. A simple diagnosis. An illness that had no cure. No good answers. Doctor after doctor, medicine after medicine, and no results. In a time when people equated long-term illness and suffering with sin, I can imagine that her friends questioned her: "What did you do to get like this?" Believing that she must be at the root of her own problem, friends unfriended her. Visits ceased. Phone calls trickled to nothing.

It was more than just the physical illness and the mental drain that weighed upon her. No matter how careful and diligent she was with her condition, the mere fact that it was occurring made her unclean. If she was married, her husband would have stopped sharing a bed with her because whatever she touched became unclean. The bed, the chair—everything in the house. Isolated and alone, this woman must have felt as if she had no one.

But she still had a glimmer of hope. She still was going to different doctors, trying new medicines and therapies in hopes that something would work. But at the same time, her money was running low. She was nearly broke.

And one day it hit her: "This isn't living," she thought. "Life isn't supposed to be like this."

While this is a hypothetical extension of what could have been this woman's life, the facts are that her sickness limited her comings and goings as well as her contact with others. Becoming a prisoner to her own home and a slave to doctors who had no answers, this woman had become worse off than when she started seeking medical help. When I read her story, I am saddened that there was no help, but I am encouraged that she did not lose hope.

You Can Change Your Situation

When I began to study this story, I realized that what this woman suffered from was not only an uncontrollable, unstoppable, unexplainable flow of blood, but also an issue of life. Blood represents life. The two are interconnected. Leviticus 17:11 and 14 tell us: "For the life of the flesh is in the blood.... For the life of every creature is its blood: its blood is its life" (ESV). In essence, life was oozing out of her body every day, and the blood that flowed was a visible confirmation that she was losing out on life, as she was helpless to change what was happening despite all her good efforts.

Have you ever felt that way? As if so much is stacked against you? And there you are with a willingness and the desire to get better, but every time you try, you end up worse off than when you started? We used to say it this way: "One step forward, three steps backward." If that's you, here are four things you can do to change your situation.

Motivate your mind.

It may sound silly to say you can motivate your mind, but the truth is that there is power in what you believe. If you believe you can do a thing, you will! Unfortunately the opposite is also true. If you believe you can't, you won't. Old mind-sets have to be challenged. And sometimes rules need to be broken. How do you begin to make an impact on your situation that can lead to change? All of it begins in your mind. As you think, so are you! (See Proverbs 23:7, KJV.) But you can't just think it; you have to put some action behind your thoughts.

Consider how bad things were for the woman. Not once does the Bible say she gave up. We aren't told that she retreated to her home to die alone of an incurable illness. To the contrary, she was actively participating in her healing. The apostle James says it like this: "Faith without works is dead" (James 2:20, NKJV). Actions help propel your faith into the realm of possibility. No matter how small or great her action, the woman was pursuing healing. She went to doctors, and when she heard Jesus was in town, she made her unthinkable decision to get to Him to be healed.

Many people I know who are facing illnesses display an immense amount of bravery that I only hope to have if I ever find myself in a similar position. Most don't even realize the amazing courage they have. Each of them has the desire to live. They are being active in the decisions for their lives and their medical care. They are an example of how we can be mentally motivated and inspired to action. The strength and courage of this nameless woman remind us that we aren't to take bad news lying down. In order to access the next level of living, we must face challenges head-on. Even if we do not get immediate answers or results, we can't give up. Be motivated to live your life.

Confront your challenges.

Instead of giving up, get up! Gather the remnants of strength you have left, and fight for your life. Fight for another opportunity, another answer, another chance to live. You may be facing a health challenge or some other fight that seems too hard for you to face alone. Why give up? You must learn to ask God for strength to endure. Never think you are alone. The Bible reminds us that in our weakness God's strength is perfected. In other words, when we are weak, He is strong for us (2 Cor. 12:9).

Push through no matter how crowded the path to victory seems. There are a plethora of reasons people fail, but the most tragic is that they didn't try. We are told that only trying can beat a failure. Don't allow things you could have or would have done become things you should have done. Do you realize how easy it is to think or talk ourselves out of a miracle? Too frequently we overthink a situation and fail to take any action. Imagine if the woman had allowed thoughts about how crowded it was going to be to keep her from going to see Jesus. Her determination led to her deliverance! Push through, no matter what.

Face your fear.

Every big challenge in our lives will be met with a certain amount of fear. It's human. But you cannot allow that to stop you. The Bible says, "God has not given us a spirit of fear, but of power, and of love, and of a sound mind" (2 Tim. 1:7, NKJV). Pray that God will change your fear into power. Face fear head-on. You will see results—it's guaranteed. Sure, the woman was fearful, but she pressed through the crowd anyway, and the trajectory of her life changed completely the moment she touched Jesus's garment.

Own your story.

You and God are the creators of your story. All the amazing promises He has outlined for your life are, in part, dependent on you. What will you do to make them happen? It's a rare testimony that things supernaturally fall into a person's lap. However, with effort and the energy God gives you—even when you feel weak, He can make you strong—you can experience your heart's desire.

When Jesus asked, "Who touched Me?" He was aware that healing virtue had gone forth from Him. I believe He knew who had touched Him. He knew her story. But would she be willing to own it? She was in disguise, but she was still that woman with an issue. Have you ever had to act as if you aren't "you"? You try to be somebody else because being you hurts too much. You have too much stuff to deal with being you. You can dress differently, but inside you know it's still you!

Jesus said, "Who touched Me?"

Then the woman, seeing that she could not go unnoticed, came trembling and fell at his feet. In the presence of all the people, she told why she had touched him and how she had been instantly healed. Then he said to her, "Daughter, your faith has healed you. Go in peace."

—LUKE 8:47–48, NIV

Her life changed in an instant. Things lost could now be restored—all because she made the unthinkable decision to do the very thing she was banned from doing: touch. Instead of accepting life as it had been defined for her, she felt there had to be something better. She stepped out, intent on being healed.

What about you? How have you been boxed in, labeled, or marginalized? What has been keeping you from getting where you planned to go? How can you do the unthinkable and change your story?

Jesus's declaration "Your faith has healed you. Go in peace" tells us that her healing was not just physical. He changed her entire life situation. The things she needed were the things she had lost over the twelve-year period. Relationships, finances, health, mental stability—everything was placed back in its proper place. If you desire for God to do the miraculous in your life, it may be time for you to do the unthinkable.

Do the Unthinkable

Reach Out and Touch Him

Everyone tried to touch him, because healing
power went out from him, and he healed everyone.
—LUKE 6:19

As a child I remember the Sunday broadcast of the
Pentecostal church in our city. At the conclusion they
would sing, "Reach Out and Touch (Somebody's Hand)."
As a teen I would hum the tune but wonder how touching
someone's hand could make the world a better place, as
the song said. I didn't want strangers to touch me.

As I've matured, I've come to realize and value the
power of an appropriate touch. It reminds me that we
are human. As one of the five senses, touch connects us
to other people in a way the other senses don't. We crave
the power of touch. And when we magnify the touch
with intention and purpose, as the woman with the
issue did, it can be the very touch that changes our lives.

Do you need to touch the hand of the Master? As
impossible as it may sound, when you touch Him, He
releases healing for the sin-sick soul. Today do the
unthinkable, and reach for God. He's reaching for you.

CHAPTER 10

AN UNTHINKABLE POSITION
MARY AND MARTHA

*"Martha, Martha," the Lord answered, "you are worried
and upset about many things, but few things are
needed—or indeed only one. Mary has chosen what
is better, and it will not be taken away from her."*

—LUKE 10:41–42, NIV

J UST THINKING ABOUT Him brought her to tears.
First, she remembered the time at the dinner party
when He let her sit at His feet. As a woman, she wasn't
supposed to be sitting there, but He made her feel welcome, like part of the group. Other teachers would
have ostracized her, but Jesus taught her just like the
men. And His words were so captivating, as if they were
reaching deep into her soul.

Mary knew about God. She was faithful to obey His commands. But Jesus made her feel as if God was near and that He loved not just her people but *her*. She barely understood what was happening, but she wanted more of His teaching. She wanted more time sitting at His feet.

As the smell of food wafted into the air, Mary remained transfixed. She knew it was proper to get up and help her sister, Martha, in the kitchen. But there was something about being able to sit, hear, and learn from Him that was making her feel like a different woman. Even when Martha marched in, demanding that she help out, Mary couldn't bring herself to leave Him. She thought for sure the teacher would tell her to help Martha, but He didn't do that. He said she had chosen what was better. She could barely believe it. Not only had He defended her decision to sit at His feet; He also affirmed it.

That was just the first incident. Not too long afterward the teacher was again at the home she shared with her brother and sister. It was just a few days after her brother had died. How hurt and sad she had been. She felt hopeless and helpless. She was afraid of what would happen to her and Martha without Lazarus.

They called for Jesus when Lazarus got sick, but He didn't come—well, not in time. Lazarus died, and they buried him. In those first few days the smell of death nauseated her and only made her feel more hopeless. Then the teacher showed up. She could remember exactly where she was when Martha told her He was there and that He was looking for her. She ran at full speed to find Him, leaving her grieving friends behind. She ran and ran, and when she saw Him, she fell at His feet.

"Lord," she said, "if You had been here, my brother would not have died." As she wept, she looked up at Him and saw that His eyes were also filled with tears. Then He called for her brother to come forth. Lazarus had been in a tomb for four days, and she knew there would be a terrible stench. But after Jesus gave the command, there he was, walking toward them wrapped in grave clothes. Her dead brother was alive! She couldn't explain it—it was a miracle. She couldn't seem to stop the flow of tears, but her tears of sorrow had become tears of joy.

Now the tears were flowing again here at this dinner party. But they weren't tears for Lazarus; they were tears for the Rabbi. She heard Him say He would not be with them long, that He would be going away. The thought of Him leaving made her weep, and her weeping turned into worship. She broke the seal on the jar of pure and expensive oil. The sweet, musky fragrance of spikenard filled the house as she poured it on His feet. Her tears mingled with the oil as she poured out her love for Him. Without even thinking, she let down her hair and used it to dry His feet. It was as if no one else existed in that moment. Positioned at His feet, she worshipped Him.

At His Feet

Jesus visited many people's houses, but none was spoken of like the home of Mary and Martha. The sisters and their brother, Lazarus, were Jesus's friends. In their home in the town of Bethany, Jesus was able to rest and spend time encouraging those closest to Him. It was also in this home that Jesus allowed a woman to sit at His feet and be taught alongside His disciples, which was typically not permitted.[1]

In New Testament times, it was highly uncommon for a woman to be educated beyond the basics. Women, children, the poor, and those of disrepute were viewed as unimportant in first-century society.[2] It wouldn't have made sense to most people for Jesus to teach a woman. It would have seemed like a waste of time because women were considered property and their value was almost completely tied to their role within the home. A married woman was covered economically by her husband. But a woman without a husband, father, or son to care for her could become destitute. That is why Jesus often challenged His followers to take care of widows.

It seems, however, that Martha and her younger sister, Mary, were financially secure even without husbands. Theologians believe Martha was widowed since she had her own home and the Bible doesn't mention that she had a husband.[3] Because her brother, Lazarus, apparently lived in the home, it is possible that he served as the man of the house, providing for his sisters. If this was the case, it certainly makes a few things about Mary and Martha easier to understand.

For instance, the average household would not have been able to accommodate a large dinner party on short notice, but Martha seemed capable of managing a last-minute gathering even though preparing food was a time-consuming process.[4] Additionally, Mary's possession of an expensive perfume indicates that she was far from indigent. Lastly, considering Lazarus's role in the family could explain the depth of the sisters' despair at his death. They must have wondered who would care for them with their brother gone and how they would sustain their lifestyle without him.

We don't know how Jesus befriended the siblings, but when He was in Bethany it became a habit for Him to stop by their house. Martha would open her doors to Him and use her resources to let Him rest and bless people from their home. This is what was happening in Luke 10:38–42. Jesus was visiting, and Martha was working hard preparing the dinner, setting the table, and serving her guests while her sister sat listening to Jesus teach. It should have been a pleasant evening, but it quickly took a turn.

Perhaps overwhelmed by all the work that needed to be done, Martha barged into the room where Jesus and His disciples were gathered and demanded that He tell Mary to help her prepare the food. She was so focused on serving the meal that she overlooked the fact that the Bread of Life was sitting in her home. I can only believe she didn't realize what was happening in her house or who was visiting her when she said, "Lord, don't you care that my sister has left me to do the work by myself? Tell her to help me!" (Luke 10:40, NIV).

What Martha certainly missed was how much Jesus did care. Martha was busy with the food preparations. I understand that. In many communities, then and today, women are judged by their hospitality. Even today women feel pressure to be great hostesses on short notice and throw grand parties regardless of their budgets. We all know that women can talk, and in a small community, you can imagine how quickly word might get around about a bad dinner party.

I imagine Martha felt pressure to perform. Have you ever felt that? I surely have. That pressure will make you feel as if you are doing everything for everyone else and no one appreciates all your hard work. It will cause you to overspend and overexert. I have been there, and it doesn't feel good. One year I had a minor surgery a few days before Thanksgiving, and no one else made preparations for the dinner. I had hoped we'd be invited to Thanksgiving dinner, but since that didn't happen, two days post-surgery, while still feeling weak, I did my best to cook for our household and our extended family.

The next day, Black Friday, took on a new meaning for me when I found myself right back in the hospital, feeling worse than before. Frustrated and in pain, I questioned God. Why did I have to do it all by myself? Didn't anyone else care that it was a major holiday and everyone in the family would be expecting a nice dinner? I had succumbed to the pressure to perform for others rather than listening to my body say don't overdo it, and I was paying the price.

The pressure to perform will make you do more than you are able to do and then question if God cares about you when you find yourself utterly exhausted. But when you really think about it, the performance pressure is often self-inflicted, as we see in Jesus's response to Martha:

> "Martha, Martha," the Lord answered, "you are worried and upset about many things, but few things are needed—or indeed only one. Mary has

chosen what is better, and it will not be taken away from her."

—LUKE 10:41–42, NIV

GOOD OR BETTER?

Interestingly Jesus said Mary had made the "better" choice. That suggests that Martha's choice wasn't bad; it just wasn't as good as Mary's. I often think Martha gets a bad rap for her role in the dinner party because in actuality Jesus didn't condemn Martha for serving. He admonished her for being anxious and troubled about what she was doing.[5] The food could have waited. I doubt anyone would have questioned Martha had she joined her sister at Jesus's feet that evening. What would have been wrong with having a late meal?

Mary chose to spend time with Jesus because she knew He was not going to be with them long. Time is one of our most valuable resources. It's one of the few things we can never get back. How often do people regret losing valuable time with loved ones when the person dies or moves away? It seems the void is never filled. While I had quality time with my mother, what I wouldn't give to spend just another hour in her presence—not cooking, not cleaning, but just looking in her face and hearing her voice. If there is one thing you gather from this moment at Martha's house, it is that some things are a more valuable use of time than others.

Martha was busy with the dinner preparations. Having hosted many dinner gatherings, I can understand her joy and pain. On one hand, you are elated that your home is the place chosen for everyone to gather and that you can prepare something wonderful for your friends and loved ones. But on the other hand, entertaining is a lot of work.

Jesus told Martha that she was concerned with many things. Is this the life of the twenty-first century woman or what? We are chief multitaskers, supermoms, and wonder women all at the same time. When I consider the Proverbs 31 woman, I want to scream because I never feel as if I can measure up to all she accomplished. Our lives are hectic, and it seems our work is never done.

Yet the reality is that some women gauge their success by their busyness. Some women just like people to depend on them. It makes them feel needed, and that makes them feel important. But I have found that this sense of being "needed" really just makes you busier. And unfortunately busy doesn't mean successful; it just means busy.

Recently I had a coaching session with a woman who was the epitome of busy. She had three jobs and was a high-level volunteer in a ministry. She obviously was committed and dependable because a lot of people delegated to her. But she felt pulled in multiple directions, unsure of what God wanted her to do and unable to say no. When I asked her about her devotional life, she assured me that it was strong, that she was praying and reading God's Word daily. But as we talked, she began to tell me that she often would fall asleep while praying or studying the Bible.

She wasn't well rested and often felt as if she wasn't functioning at her best. Was God pleased with the fact that she overcommitted herself for the sake of ministry?

I don't think so. He wants our full attention. If we are so busy working for Him that we're not worshipping Him, we actually will miss His voice. It is in those times when your busyness has gotten out of sync that God will prune your life to become more like He wants it to be.

Have you ever been pruned by God? I have, and to be honest, it was one of the most difficult seasons of my life. In the pruning process God will cut back parts of your life, and it will look as if that area is dead. However, in time new growth will appear from those areas that have been pruned. The best part is that the new growth is healthier than what existed before the pruning. Relationships, dreams and aspirations, finances, commitments—these are all areas God can and will cut back. During seasons of pruning God will set new priorities for you. You can try to make sense of the things you have going on in your life, but the reality is that God wants to make sense of it for you. You just have to trust Him.

After I shared this with the woman I was coaching, her tears flowed. She had been feeling overwhelmed but stagnant and isolated from others in ministry. I let her know that the pruning process would usher her into her new season. She realized that with her schedule filled to the brim and every moment accounted for, she had to let some things go. That decision in itself was a major step toward progress. To allow God to prune our lives and our agendas, we must accept that He has a bigger and better plan that we don't always see. That means we can't hold on to things when God is trying to lighten our load. This woman had to trust that God's pruning was not just taking away, but He was making a way for her because she was too busy to do what He wanted her to do.

If you are feeling a sense of stagnation, perhaps it is for the same reason. God can't grow you when you have too much going on and you aren't focused on Him. When He cuts back the excess that is no longer necessary or that is hindering you in life, then and only then will you experience tremendous growth. Imagine if both Mary and Martha had been positioned at Jesus's feet. They would have become powerhouse women disciples! Martha had the opportunity to make a better choice, but she missed it because she was too preoccupied. Don't miss out on the better part.

Martha is mentioned three times in the Scriptures: in Luke 10, when she felt overwhelmed working alone at the dinner party; in John 11, when she met Jesus after her brother died; and in John 12 at a dinner six days before the Passover. When we encounter her in this last setting, we see a different Martha.

> Six days before the Passover celebration began, Jesus arrived in Bethany, the home of Lazarus—the man he had raised from the dead. A dinner was prepared in Jesus' honor. Martha served, and Lazarus was among those who ate with him. Then Mary took a twelve-ounce jar of expensive perfume made from essence of nard, and she anointed Jesus' feet with it, wiping his feet with her hair. The house was filled with the fragrance.
> —JOHN 12:1–3

You might be thinking, "But Martha's still serving. What changed?" Yes, she's still serving, but this time she is serving with a different perspective. She is serving with the heart of a worshipper. She isn't complaining that Mary isn't helping her, nor is she complaining about the amount of work she has to do. She is serving with joy! I believe her change of heart happened after Lazarus's death.

When Martha saw Jesus after Lazarus died, her conversation had a similar tone to the one in Luke 10 when she complained to Jesus that Mary wasn't helping her. When Jesus arrived at their home, Martha seemed to blame Jesus for her brother's death, saying, "Lord, if only you had been here, my brother would not have died" (John 11:21).

But then her conversation shifted when she said, "But even now I know that God will give you whatever you ask" (John 11:22). In that moment she demonstrated great faith because the only way to get Lazarus back at that point was for Jesus to raise the dead. Taking her words seriously, Jesus then asked her if she believed in Him, saying, "I am the resurrection and the life. Anyone who believes in me will live, even after dying. Everyone who lives in me and believes in me will never ever die. Do you believe this, Martha?" (John 11:25–26).

She replied: "Yes, Lord...I have always believed you are the Messiah, the Son of God, the one who has come into the world from God" (John 11:27). Notice that she was quick to affirm her faith in Jesus as the Christ and to acknowledge His ability to raise the dead. That level of faith only comes from learning of Christ, which comes from staying close to Him. In her second encounter with Christ, Martha no longer questioned *if* He cared. Now she is affirming that He is the Messiah, the Son of God, who had come into the world. Martha had grown. Her response to Jesus was a bold declaration of a new level of faith.

DON'T DEVALUE THE PROCESS

Pruning leads to growth, but you also have to be an active part of the process. Martha experienced growth because she very likely made adjustments in her life. She wasn't just pruned in order to be left looking barren. She was pruned so she could experience growth. When we remove the small things from our lives that drain us of time and energy, we free up space and time to do the things that matter most. When we learn to release the things that can be delegated, it frees us up to be used in other areas that we should be developing.

If your plate is too full, you need to remove some things. In order for God to open the right opportunity for you at the right time, you must be available to Him. In essence, you must also be accountable for this growth. Don't expect that God will empty your agenda and responsibilities without having a bigger purpose in mind. It is important that you sense when He wants you to make the adjustments. Being overwhelmed is just one way of knowing that you are doing too much! I have learned that there is power in the word *no*. If you want to be polite, you can say, "No, I cannot make that commitment at this time." However you say it, you need to learn to release yourself from overcommitting and under-delivering.

The fact is that we are busy people who are surrounded by busy people. Everyone seems to be living a hectic life, so much so that if you don't seem as busy as the next person, you might think something is wrong with you. We are so busy that it can be difficult to know what to do when we have free time! I often find myself filling up those times with things I hadn't gotten to because, of course, I was too busy.

But as much as we complain about our fast-paced lives, the truth is we like being busy. We think somehow that the busier we are, the more special we are because the work we do is so valuable that no one else can do it, or at least not the way we do it. Busy people are usually effective people. We look to them when we need something done because they are generally good at what they do and are dependable. But the problem isn't just that we're busy; it's what we are so busy doing.

When our agendas are completely filled, we have little room for growth and little room for God. Some of us are too busy to do anything new. What if that new thing is the one thing that could lead you to your life's purpose? Are you too exhausted to even consider it? God wants to blow your mind. As Ephesians 3:20 says, He wants to do more than you can ask or imagine! But will you be too tired or frustrated to recognize or receive it? In Luke 10 Jesus Christ was sitting in Martha's living room, and she was in the kitchen. He was sharing a life-giving, life-altering message with His disciples, and He wanted to share it with her too, but she was too occupied with the busywork of life.

When I was a kid, my mother worked two and sometimes three jobs out of necessity. She would leave our home at 7:30 in the morning, only to return for forty-five minutes in the early evening, change clothes, make sure there was dinner for us, and go to her part-time evening job. She'd return home around 9:45 p.m. and get up and do the same thing the next day. For a while she worked a third part-time job that had her at work until 11:30 p.m. There were some days when we really only saw her for a few moments in the morning before school and for the forty-five minutes when she was home before she went to her second job.

On the days she had off, she still was busy. While we sat and watched a television show or a movie, Mom would be cooking or cleaning, always in motion. It's hard to believe, but as much as I disliked her busyness, at a certain point in my life I realized that I'd become much like my mother! There were many times when my family would be watching a TV show, and laughter filled the air as I sat at my computer working or was in the kitchen cooking or cleaning. There was always something to do, and someone had to do it.

I finally learned to value the present moment, to be in the "now." It took my youngest son saying, "Mom, you aren't listening. You are typing on the computer," to get my attention. He was right. He was talking to me, and I was multitasking, as I usually did. When my son said those words to me, I heard the voice of God saying,

"Your son needs you now, not later." I stopped and apologized to him and looked in his eyes as he talked to me.

That was a turning point in my life. God did a bit of a pruning to help me see an area of my life that I needed to improve. My sons were not going to live with me forever. They would graduate from high school and go away to college. If the foundation of true communication had never been laid, I wouldn't have the relationship with them that I have today. We talk. We listen. We laugh. We cry. We love. We aren't too busy for one another.

Like Martha, I had assumed that serving was more important than spending time. But I now know that the better choice was to spend time being with my family rather than simply doing things for them. Too often we think doing for God is more important than being with God. Or we get the two—doing and being with—mixed up. There is a difference. We can be so busy working for God that we miss out on worshipping Him. Many church leaders and ministry workers are misguided by the thought that serving is their act of worship. Serving is service; it isn't worship. It is important to differentiate between the two. Can we worship God through our service? I say only in part because when we are serving, we are often thinking of others and how we can help them. Our heart is directed toward pleasing God, but our focus is on meeting the needs of those around us.

We are in the worship service, but our minds are distracted, so we often leave still hungry for God's presence. Even if your heart is in the right place, it is difficult to worship and serve at the same time. This is why it is important that those who serve in the church, in any capacity, make time to worship God. It may have to take place outside the church service, but it must be a priority. I believe ministry burnout is so common because so few leaders actually sit at the feet of Jesus. What we do *with* Christ is what prepares us for what we do *for* Christ.

As Jesus said, "Martha, Martha, you are worried about many things, but Mary has chosen the better part."

LIFE IS ABOUT CHOICES

Each believer is given a choice to be a worker or a worshipper. But here's the thing: most worshippers will learn to become effective workers. Being in the presence of God will move you to action. I love the way *Experiencing God* author Henry Blackaby puts it: we must find out what God is doing and seek to join Him.[6] When you are experiencing God, you will not want to be fed and just sit there full of His blessings. You will want to share! God doesn't want lazy people in His flock. He wants us to be at work. The good news is that once you learn to worship properly, you will learn to work expediently. Servants all need an occasional reminder that God wants us to be like Mary and sit at His feet. Only after we have spent time in His presence will He send us out as Marthas to do His work.

What's your priority? Mary chose what was best. In life we will be presented with choices, and our choices will determine our life outcomes. The key to making good choices is setting the right priorities. When we make

God our first priority, our perspective and all our other responsibilities will fall into place, like pieces of a puzzle.

Mary sat at Jesus's feet, and Martha criticized her. Later, Mary poured expensive oil on Jesus's feet, and Judas criticized her, saying the oil should have been sold and the money given to the poor. Sure, the oil was valuable, possibly worth a year's wages for a common laborer.[7] But wasn't Jesus worth it? Mary thought so.

Jesus felt Mary had her priorities in line, which is why He corrected both of the people who ridiculed her. The oil Mary poured on Jesus was a sacrificial offering of worship made to her Lord. Centuries later we still recall what Mary did, and we celebrate her worship as an example to emulate because it was pure, free, and fully focused on Christ.

When Mary was attacked for worshipping Jesus so extravagantly, He defended her, saying her gift was needed because it was preparation for His burial. This reminds me of how some people still react to the unthinkable worship that true worshippers offer to God. To onlookers the worship seems excessive and foolish, but to the worshipper it is necessary.

From time to time people will ask me: "Why pray when things are still bad?" "Why go to church when life is spiraling out of control?" "Why give tithes when money is tight?" "Why even believe God?" People have so many questions regarding the *whys* of our relationship with God. However, the person with the heart of a worshipper knows the answers to those questions. It is because He is worth it! To be in His presence, to sense His glory, to feel His awesomeness—that all begins with a choice. Mary chose to worship Jesus. And because He was her priority, He blessed her with His presence. What will you choose? I choose as Mary did; I choose God.

POSITIONED FOR PURPOSE

Mary's choices always led to her being properly positioned for a purposeful interaction with Jesus. In his *Bible Exposition Commentary*, Warren Wiersbe notes that each time Mary is mentioned in Luke and John, "she is in the same place: at the feet of Jesus. She sat at His feet and listened to His Word (Luke 10:39), fell at His feet and shared her woe (John 11:32), and came to His feet and poured out her worship (John 12:3)."[8] Each time she was positioned at Jesus's feet, her interaction with Him caused her to do or receive exactly what was needed in that moment.

Sitting at Jesus's feet in Luke 10

During a banquet in ancient Israel people would usually be found seated upon chairs or lounging on couches. But when Jesus was present, His disciples would sit at His feet and listen to their teacher. Mary clearly did the unthinkable when she positioned herself as a disciple, one who sought to learn from Jesus. Her position increased not only her love for Jesus but also her understanding of His message. She listened, and she learned, and because she took that position, she was prepared to share the gospel when the time was right.

Falling at Jesus's feet in John 11

Falling at Jesus's feet after her brother Lazarus died, Mary gave Jesus her burdens, pains, hurts, and fears. Like her sister, Mary said, "Lord, if only you had been here, my brother would not have died" (John 11:32). When Martha said them, they seemed to be words of criticism or complaint. But when we read that statement in light of Mary's position at Jesus's feet, we see them as words spoken in confidence and love. I think if the Bible had pictured her running to Jesus, standing face-to-face with Him, and saying the very same words, we would have a different sense of her tone and the intent of her words. But knowing that she was at His feet, the right position to share her grief and sorrow, causes us to see her differently. We see her humility and her faith in His power and authority.

Mary's position got Jesus's attention. Jesus felt her pain. He loved her brother too; in fact, Lazarus's death is the only time Scripture says Jesus wept. When Mary looked up at Him, she saw the tears in His eyes. Can you imagine how it must have felt for her to know that He understood her pain and sorrow? Jesus saw her and knew what she felt, and it was His compassion for her that moved Him to action to call Lazarus forth.

Worshipping at Jesus's feet in John 12

A few days before the Passover celebration Jesus returned to Bethany and had dinner with Mary, Martha, and Lazarus. Once again, Mary positioned herself at Jesus's feet. This time it wasn't to sit and learn, nor to fall in sorrow, but to pour out her love to Him. In a sacrificial and humble act she poured expensive oil on His feet and then wiped them with her hair. In this time period, it was unheard of for a Jewish woman to let down her hair. Yet as Warren Wiersbe notes, "When she came to the feet of Jesus, Mary took the place of a slave....She humbled herself and laid her glory at His feet."[9]

Mary may not have even realized in that moment how powerful her actions were, but there was a great purpose in them. Every culture has customs surrounding burial, including the ancient Israelites. They would prepare the body with spices and oils, reflecting their belief in an afterlife.[10] After Jesus's death at Calvary, Joseph of Arimathea and Nicodemus hurriedly took His body, wrapped it in linen cloths and spices, and then placed Him in a tomb. Because it was the Sabbath when no work could be done, they were unable to prepare his body for a proper burial. (See John 19:38–40.) It was Mary's unexpected offering while Jesus was alive that readied His body.

Still today Jesus wants us to choose what is better and position ourselves humbly before Him. Spiritually this means choosing a relationship with God over the busyness of life. When we intentionally spend time with God, we get to know His Word and His ways and are empowered to do His work. This sometimes means we will make sacrifices that others cannot understand, but as Mary realized, our God is worth the sacrifice.

Positioning ourselves before Him in the natural means staying open to His pruning so we can continue to grow. Previously I spoke about a woman in ministry whom God was pruning. When she realized she had too much to do and that she could not grow in her busy space, she delegated some of the work, and God opened new doors for her as a result.

If you feel frustrated with where you are in life or as if you're not growing, you may not be positioned properly. You may need to reprioritize, reorganize, and delegate some things in your life so you can shift into the right position and begin to grow.

When we are in the right position, God can change our situations overnight. I call it instant elevation. It takes only a second for God to place you on someone's heart who could change your life in a matter of minutes—one phone call, one email, one mention of your name, one viral YouTube video, a one-second exposure of your gift to the right person. But you can miss those opportunities if you are out of position. There may be an opening at work that seems impossible for you to get when you consider your credentials. But when you are positioned properly, God can influence people to make decisions that will open doors for you! Being in the right position at the right time will make all the difference in the world.

Unlike some of the stories in this book, Mary did not come to the Lord in dire need or a crisis. She came with a desire. That desire was to learn, grow, and become more like Him. And the Lord rewarded the unthinkable priority she set and the unthinkable position she took at His feet.

More concerned with performance than her position, Martha was rebuked for being worried about everything except that which was most important. But as Martha progressed, she shifted her attitude about her service. I believe she refocused her energy not on what she was doing but on why she was doing it.

As I prayed this morning, I began to consider if my prayers were laden with work for God or love for God. Was I only asking God to meet my needs and help me accomplish my to-do list? Or was I seeking Him? Was I thanking Him for being my God and my help? I don't want to seek God for what He can do for me. He already has done so much. Worshipping Him allows us to experience the fullness of His Spirit in our lives and receive the strength and power to accomplish any task. As I've shifted my priorities and my position to truly seek God, I have received His power and His peace.

The apostle Paul told the early church, "Keep putting into practice all you learned and received from me—everything you heard from me and saw me doing. Then the God of peace will be with you" (Phil. 4:9). As you spend more time with God, you will experience the peace of God. Is it time to rethink your priorities and shift your position?

DO THE UNTHINKABLE

Get Closer to God

> Come close to God, and God will come close to you.
>
> —JAMES 4:8

What is more important, doing for God or being with God? It seems the answer would be easy, but sometimes the lines can get blurry. Never forget that God wants our full attention. The writer of Ecclesiastes said, "For everything there is a season, a time for every activity under heaven" (Eccles. 3:1). Recognizing the right time to be with God is important.

If you are one of the Marthas of this world, it may seem unthinkable to stop your work to sit and learn at Jesus's feet. But as He said, it is the better choice. Know in your heart that sitting with Jesus, spending time with Him each day, is more necessary than anything else you will do with your time. If you are like Mary, then you already value the importance of spending time drawing near to God. Maintain that commitment. Don't let the cares of life cause you to change positions.

Determine to know the position you must be in so you may receive from Him. As you spend time with Him, you will receive the infilling of His Spirit, the joy of His presence, and the power of His Word. He will prepare you to be a vessel that pours out His amazing love to others.

CONCLUSION

*Now to Him who is able to do exceedingly
abundantly above all that we ask or think,
according to the power that works in us.*

—EPHESIANS 3:20, NKJV

T'S AMAZING WHAT God can do with the smallest
things. One step, one touch, one conversation, one
unthinkable sacrifice can change your life. If you just
reach out to God by taking even a tiny step of faith, He
can do the impossible.

As I was writing this book, something unexpected
happened. I am no stranger to taking steps of faith. As
I've shared in these pages, I walked into the unknown
when I decided to leave my corporate job and ultimately follow God's call to preach the gospel. But as I
was writing, I sensed God challenging me to look in the
mirror. There were areas of my life where He wanted to
bring change. There were new things He wanted to do,

new dreams He wanted to fulfill. And in order for them to come to pass, I would have to break some old mindsets that were keeping me bound to life "as is."

God has big dreams for you. He has placed desires in your heart that only He can make a reality. And believe it or not, the devil is not the biggest obstacle. Neither are your circumstances. The biggest challenge is you. God wants to expand your world. But in order for that to happen, you must let Him remove the things that keep you from doing something bigger and better. He wants to get rid of the voices telling you to play it safe instead of stepping out in faith. He wants to destroy the belief that your life will never change, that your situation will never be different. He wants to remove every obstacle keeping you from doing the unthinkable and experiencing the extraordinary.

We are all facing change. Whether we initiate the change, as the woman with the alabaster jar did, or something happens in life that forces us to make a change, as happened to Ruth and Naomi, there will be times in all our lives when we will need to do something we never thought to do before. When you face those crossroads, you can either sabotage yourself and your future by refusing to change, or, like the daughters of Zelophehad, Abigail, and Rahab, you can step beyond your prescribed boundaries and soar into something you never thought possible.

Un-think-able. When we break this word down into its parts, we really get a feel for what God wants us to do. We are *able* to *think*, but we've limited ourselves by placing "un" in front of the word. God wants to do more than we can ask for or think of, but we have an enemy who doesn't even want us to think about what God is able to do in and through us. He wants us to see only the "un" and not the "thinkable." But let that mind-set end today. I want you to challenge every single thing that has limited you—the things people said you could not do, the places where they said you could not go, the dreams and desires they said you could not have. Joseph saw his dreams come true against incredible odds, and so can you.

Do something revolutionary, and start to think about the dreams that have long been buried. See yourself living in the reality of those dreams. Even if you can't fathom it, God can. When you take the limits off God, you take the limits off yourself!

Think about it. Throughout the Bible, God used women such as Mary and Martha, the woman at the well, and the woman with the issue of blood to participate in bringing people to salvation. Through Eve humanity was birthed. Through Mary our salvation through Jesus Christ was birthed. God wants to birth miracles through you. God accomplishes the unordinary through people just like you and me, and our lives give witness to His extraordinary power. All we must do is allow His power to work in and through us.

What will you do that has been unthinkable? Challenge your life, your actions, and your mind-set. It is my prayer that you rediscover long-buried desires, dreams, and purpose. As you encounter the hidden desires of your heart, you will once again see with the eyes of faith to overcome limits that were placed on those dreams.

By recognizing His ability to overcome your limits, you will, in fact, be pleasing God, and that will bring His rewards in your life. Hebrews 11:6 says, "And it is impossible to please God without faith. Anyone who wants to come to him must believe that God exists and that he rewards those who sincerely seek him." Your faith will open the door to realizing your dreams!

Will you consider how things could be? Will you dream once again? Do not allow your dreams to die. Forgive. Be courageous. Believe. Commit. Be wise. Be blessed. Reach out. Sacrifice. Speak. And position yourself for greatness. The extraordinary can be yours.

NOTES

Introduction

1.   *Oxford Living Dictionaries*, s.v. "unthinkable," accessed November 4, 2017, https://en.oxforddictionaries.com /definition/unthinkable.

Chapter 1: Unthinkable Trust

1.   *Merriam-Webster's Dictionary*, s.v. "trust," accessed October 23, 2017, https://www.merriam-webster.com /dictionary/trust.

2.   Jonathan Bernis, *Unlocking the Prophetic Mysteries of Israel* (Lake Mary, FL: Charisma House, 2017), 12.

3.   Bernis, *Unlocking the Prophetic Mysteries of Israel*, 12–13.

4.   National Aeronautics and Space Administration, "Measuring the Distance," accessed November 13, 2017, https:// www.nasa.gov/audience/foreducators/k-4/features/F _Measuring_the_Distance_Student_Pages.html.

Chapter 2: An Unthinkable Conversation

1.   J. M. Freeman and H. J. Chadwick, *Manners and Customs of the Bible* (North Brunswick, NJ: Bridge-Logos Publishers, 1998), 514.

2.   John D. Barry, ed., *The Lexham Bible Dictionary* (Bellingham, WA: Lexham Press, 2016), s.v. "Samaritans."

3.   Whether married or single, women were not to be saluted or spoken to in the streets, and they certainly were not to be instructed in the law. Craig S. Keener, *The IVP Bible Background Commentary: New Testament* (Downers Grove, IL: InterVarsity Press, 1993), s.v. "John 4:27–30."

Chapter 3: Unthinkable Courage

1.   Judson Cornwall and Stelman Smith, *The Exhaustive Dictionary of Bible Names* (North Brunswick, NJ: Bridge-Logos, 1998), 164.

2.   Cornwall and Smith, The Exhaustive Dictionary of Bible Names, 186.

3.   Amanda MacMillan, "12 Reasons to Stop Multitasking Now!," Health.com, accessed November 13, 2017, http://www .health.com/health/gallery/0,,20707868,00.html#you-re-not -actually-good-at-it-0.

4.   Cornwall and Smith, The Exhaustive Dictionary of Bible Names, 105.

5.   Arin Murphy-Hiscock, Birds—A Spiritual Field Guide: Explore the Symbology and Significance of These Divine Winged Messengers (New York: Simon and Schuster, 2011), 141–142.

6.   George Paxton, Illustrations of the Holy Scriptures: In Three Parts, Volume 2 (Edinburgh: Stirling and Kenney, 1825), 316–138.

7.   Blue Letter Bible, s.v. "Milcah," accessed November 13, 2017, https://www.blueletterbible.org/lang/Lexicon/Lexicon .cfm?strongs=H4435&t=KJV.

8.   Cornwall and Smith, The Exhaustive Dictionary of Bible Names, 175.

9.   Cornwall and Smith, The Exhaustive Dictionary of Bible Names, 239.

10.   Cheri Fuller and Jennifer Kennedy Dean, The One Year Praying the Promises of God (Grand Rapids, MI: Tyndale House Publishers, 2012), 92.

Chapter 4: Unthinkable Wisdom

1.   "Do Opposites Attract?," eHarmony, accessed November 13, 2017, http://www.eharmony.com/dating-advice /dating/do-opposites-attract/#.WdRDvWhSzIU.

2.   *Gesenius's Hebrew and Chaldee Lexicon*, s.v. "Nabal," accessed October 5, 2017, https://www.blueletterbible.org/lang /Lexicon/Lexicon.cfm?strongs=H5037&t=KJV.

3. "All the Women of the Bible—Abigail," Bible Gateway, accessed November 13, 2017, https://www.biblegateway.com /resources/all-women-bible/Abigail.

4. "All the Women of the Bible—Abigail." Bible Gateway,

5. *Oxford Living Dictionaries, s.v.* "humility," accessed November 13, 2017, https://en.oxforddictionaries.com /definition/us/humility.

6. *Oxford Living Dictionaries, s.v.* "pride," accessed November 13, 2017, https://en.oxforddictionaries.com /definition/us/pride.

Chapter 5: Unthinkable Belief

1. Blue Letter Bible, s.v. "Zanah," accessed November 13, 2017, https://www.blueletterbible.org/lang/Lexicon/Lexicon .cfm?strongs=H2181&t=KJV.

2. Bible Gateway, "All the Women of the Bible—Rahab," accessed November 13, 2017, https://www.biblegateway.com /resources/all-women-bible/Rahab.

3. *Encyclopaedia Britannica,* s.v. "Baal," accessed November 13, 2017, https://www.britannica.com/topic/Baal -ancient-deity.

4. Bible Gateway, "All the Women of the Bible—Rahab."

5. Rita Hancock, *Radical Well-Being* (Lake Mary, FL: Siloam, 2013), 238–239

Chapter 6: Unthinkable Commitment

1. Jerram Barrs, *Through His Eyes: God's Perspective on Women in the Bible* (Wheaton, IL: Crossway Books, 2009), 124–125.

2. Blue Letter Bible, s.v. "Naomi," accessed November 13, 2017, https://www.blueletterbible.org/lang/Lexicon/Lexicon .cfm?strongs=H5281&t=KJV.

3. Blue Letter Bible, s.v. "Mahlon," accessed November 13, 2017, https://www.blueletterbible.org/lang/Lexicon/Lexicon .cfm?strongs=H4248&t=KJV.

4. Blue Letter Bible, s.v. "Ruth," accessed November 13, 2017, https://www.blueletterbible.org/lang/Lexicon/Lexicon .cfm?strongs=H7327&t=KJV.

5. *Merriam-Webster's Dictionary*, s.v. "mentor," accessed November 13, 2017, https://www.merriam-webster.com /dictionary/mentor.

6. Bible Study Tools, s.v. "Kinsman-Redeemer," accessed November 13, 2017, http://www.biblestudytools.com /dictionaries/bakers-evangelical-dictionary/kinsman-redeemer .html.

7. Blue Letter Bible, s.v. "ga'al," accessed November 13, 2017, https://www.blueletterbible.org/lang/Lexicon/Lexicon .cfm?strongs=H1350&t=KJV.

8. Albert Barnes, "Commentary on Psalm 37:5," Barnes' Notes on the New Testament, accessed October 27, 2017, https://www.studylight.org/commentary/psalms/37-5.html.

Chapter 7: Unthinkable Worship

1. Merriam-Webster's Dictionary, s.v. "faith," accessed January 4, 2018, https://www.merriam-webster.com/dictionary/ faith.

2. BibleGateway.com, Genesis 27:36, New Living Translation, footnote, accessed November 14, 2017, https:// www.biblegateway.com/passage/?search=Gen%2027%3A36 &version=NLT.

3. BibleGateway.com, 1 Chronicles 4:9, New Living Translation, footnote, accessed November 14, 2017, https:// www.biblegateway.com/passage/?search=1+Chronicles+4%3A9 &version=NLT.

4. Blue Letter Bible, s.v. "metamorphoō," accessed November 13, 2017, https://www.blueletterbible.org/lang /Lexicon/Lexicon.cfm?strongs=G3339&t=KJV.

5. Merriam-Webster's Dictionary, s.v. "metamorphosis," accessed November 13, 2017, https://www.merriam-webster .com/dictionary/metamorphosis.

6. Craig S. Keener, *The IVP Bible Background Commentary: New Testament* (Downers Grove, IL: InterVarsity Press, 1993), s.v. "Luke 7."

7. *Encyclopaedia Britannica*, s.v. "gypsum," accessed November 13, 2017, https://www.britannica.com/science /gypsum.

8. Penny Starr, "Pornography Use among Self-Identified Christians Largely Mirrors National Average, Survey Finds," CNSNews.com, accessed November 13, 2017, http://www .cnsnews.com/news/article/penny-starr/pornography-use -among-self-identified-christians-largely-mirrors-national.

9. Laurie Morrissey, "Snakes Can Smell With Forked Tongue," *Burlington Free Press*, accessed November 13, 2017, http://www.burlingtonfreepress.com/story/news/local/2016 /05/13/snakes-can-smell-forked-tongue/84284976/.

CHAPTER 8: UNTHINKABLE FORGIVENESS

1. Zaphenath-paneah probably means "God speaks and lives." *Holy Bible: New Living Translation* (Carol Stream, IL: Tyndale House Publishers, 2013), 41:45a.

2. Mayo Clinic, "Forgiveness: Letting Go of Grudges and Bitterness," accessed November 13, 2017, http://www .mayoclinic.org/healthy-lifestyle/adult-health/in-depth /forgiveness/art-20047692.

3. As quoted by Suryalee Athwaria and A. K. Srivastava, "Forgiveness: The Way to Holistic Well-Being," *The International Journal of Indian Psychology*, vol. 3, iss. 4 (Gujarat, India: IJIP, 2016), 30.

4. Blue Letter Bible, s.v. "Manasseh," accessed November 13, 2017, https://www.blueletterbible.org/lang/Lexicon/Lexicon .cfm?strongs=H4519&t=KJV.

5. Blue Letter Bible, s.v. "Ephraim," accessed November 13, 2017, https://www.blueletterbible.org/lang/Lexicon/Lexicon .cfm?strongs=H669&t=KJV.

CHAPTER 10: AN UNTHINKABLE POSITION

1. Craig S. Keener, *The IVP Bible Background Commentary: New Testament* (Downers Grove, IL: InterVarsity Press, 1993), s.v. "Luke 10:39."

2. L. O. Richards, *The Bible Reader's Companion* (Wheaton, IL: Victor Books, 1991), 649.

3. Walter A. Elwell and Philip W. Comfort, editors, *Tyndale Bible Dictionary* (Wheaton, IL: Tyndale House Publishers, 2001), 864.

4.   John D. Barry, ed., *Faithlife Study Bible* (Bellingham, WA: Lexham Press, 2016).

5.   John D. Barry, ed., *Faithlife Study Bible.*

6.   Polly House, "Blackaby's 'Experiencing God': 15 Years of Seeing God Work," Baptist Press, accessed October 16, 2017, http://www.blackaby.net/expgod/2010/12/02/blackabys-%E2%8 0%98experiencing-god%E2%80%99-15-years-of-seeing-god -work/.

7.   Warren W. Wiersbe, *The Bible Exposition Commentary*, vol. 1 (Wheaton, IL: Victor Books, 1996), 339.

8.   Warren W. Wiersbe, *The Bible Exposition Commentary*, vol. 1, 213.

9.   Warren W. Wiersbe, *The Bible Exposition Commentary*, vol. 1, 339.

10.   John D. Barry, ed., *The Lexham Bible Dictionary* (Bellingham, WA: Lexham Press, 2016), s.v. "burial."